Zacharias Tanee Fomum

The Ministry Of Praise
And Thanksgiving

Christian Publishing House

The Ministry Of Praise
And Thanksgiving

By
ZACHARIAS TANEE FOMUM

CHRISTIAN PUBLISHING HOUSE
B.P. 7100 YAOUNDE - CAMEROUN

© 1992, Z.T. FOMUM

I Gladly Dedicate This Book To

DONALD NGONGE

A Man Of God And A Man Of Prayer
In The Making

TABLE OF CONTENTS

Preface

PART THREE: DAVID AND THE MINISTRY OF PRAISE AND THANKSGIVING

PART FOUR: COSTLY PRAISE AND THANKSGIVING

PART FIVE: THE PRACTICE OF PRAISE

PREFACE

This book, THE MINISTRY OF PRAISE AND THANKSGIVING, is the eighth in the series: «The Prayer Life.» The books in this series that have already been written are:

1. The Way Of Victorious Praying

2. The Ministry Of Fasting

3. The Art Of Intercession

4. The Practice Of Intercession

5. With Christ In The School And Ministry Of Praying

6. Moving God Through Prayer

7. Practical Spiritual Warfare Through Prayer

8. **The Ministry Of Praise And Thanksgiving**

9. Waiting On The Lord In Prayer

10. The Ministry Of Supplication

11. Life-Changing Thoughts On Prayer,
    Volume 1

12. The Centrality Of Prayer

13. Spiritual Aggressiveness

Praise and Thanksgiving are musts for the maturing believer. Praise and Thanksgiving are the exaltation of God: The Father, the Son and the Holy Spirit. There are aspects of intercourse with God in which a man seeks to ask and receive from the Lord. These asking and receiving aspects of prayer are primarily man centred. A man comes to the Lord with a need and asks and receives from the Lord. The Lord is glad to give, but man is the direct beneficiary.

However, in Praise and Thanksgiving, a man forgets his needs and comes to the Lord, receives a revelation of the Person or a deed of the Lord, and then praises and thanks the Lord for who He is or for what He has done. God is thus the object of the Ministry of Praise and Thanksgiving! God's heart is satisfied. His «need» of praise and thanksgiving is met. He is exalted and His heart satisfied.

God demands that the saints render this ministry to Him

unceasingly. He wants praise from His own round the
clock. He is glad when praise flows from His to Him. He is
disappointed when it does not come.

The believer is called to praise and thank the Lord unceasingly
- always, at all times and in every circumstance. It is as if
God were saying to the believer, «Forget yourself, forget
your circumstances; praise and thank Me. Praise and thank
Me when you like what has happened. Praise and thank Me
when you see the good in what I have done. Praise and thank
Me when you do not see any good in what has happened. I
am sovereign. That which has happened, which is apparently
good, I will cause to work out for your blessing. That which
has happened and is apparently bad, I will cause to work out
for your blessing. As long as you remain yielded to Me, I
will cause all that has happened to you to turn out for your
blessing. I have willed good for you and what I have willed
for you will come to pass, regardless of what may apparently
be happening.»

In the call to praise and thanksgiving at all times and in all
circumstances, the Lord is saying to those who know and love
Him, «My children, all will work out for your good. Do not
look only at the immediate circumstances. Do not look only
at the here and now. Look ahead. Look fifty or one hundred
years ahead, and then you will see that this apparent tragedy

has been moulded into a blessing for you by Me. I know what I am doing. All will be as it should be. The future will hold together. Show that you believe that I am in control; show that you believe that I am sovereign, show that you believe that I am able to transform the ugliest event into a blessing for you, by praising and thanking Me now in every circumstance, even though you do not yet know how I will work in this circumstance for your blessing! Have faith in Me. Believe Me now, in spite of the present situation, for what I will do in the future!

Believing God now and trusting all the future to Him, everyone who loves the Lord should act his faith by now obeying the command of the Lord which says, «*Rejoice always, pray constantly, give thanks in all circumstances; for this is the will of God in Christ Jesus for you. Do not quench the Spirit*» (1 Thessalonians 5:16 19 RSV), and also the Scripture which says, «*Always giving thanks to God the Father for everything, in the name of our Lord Jesus Christ*» (Ephesians 5:20).

There will be many events for which you will immediately cry out, «Praise the Lord!" because you see the immediate benefit to you from what has happened. Ensure that that cry is loud, firm and unceasing.

There will be other events which, on immediate analysis, seem to be bad or very bad for you. Also cry out, «Praise the Lord!»

even though you do not see any immediate benefit that can come out of them. Cry out, «Praise the Lord!» Ensure that the cry is loud, firm and unceasing. God has willed that you thus praise Him. Do. He will act and you will be amazed by the way He will transform apparent tragedies into great blessings.

Glory be to the Lord !

I will be glad to hear from you as to the impact and outflow of this message in your life and through your life.

Zacharias TANEE FOMUM,
P.O. Box 6090,
Yaounde, Cameroon.

PART ONE

PRAISE
AND
THANKSGIVING

THE MINISTRY OF PRAISE AND THANKSGIVING

1. THE MINISTRY OF PRAISE AND THANKSGIVING

The Ministry of Praise and Thanksgiving is the flowing forth of gratitude through the lips to the Lord God: The Father, the Son and the Holy Spirit, for the following:

01.   All that He was in eternity past.
02.   All the He has been in time past.
03.   All that He is at the present time.
04.   All that He will be in the future.
05.   All that He will be in eternity to come.
06.   All that He did in eternity past.
07.   All that He did in time past.
08.   All that He is doing at the present time.
09.   All that He will do in the time that is coming ahead.
10.   All that He will do in eternity to come.

So Praise and Thanksgiving involve the flowing forth in gratitude through the lips to God for His Person in the past, in the present and in the future; and for His deeds in the past, in the present and in the future.

It is possible to distinguish praise from thanksgiving by limiting praise to gratitude for whom God was, is and will be, and then having thanksgiving as the flowing forth of gratitude for what God did, is doing and will do. <u>On that distinction, praise is thanksgiving for His Person, His Being;</u>

<u>while thanksgiving is praise for His acts.</u>

We can represent the Ministry of Praise as follows:

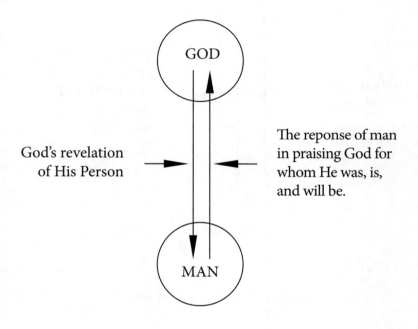

God's revelation of His Person

The reponse of man in praising God for whom He was, is, and will be.

The ministry of praise

We can represent the Ministry of Thanksgiving as follows:

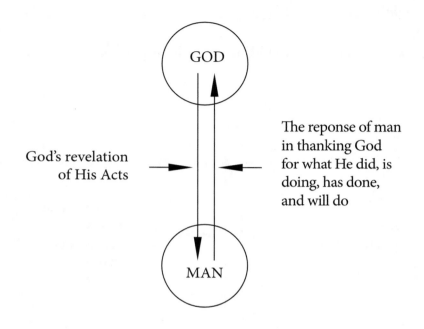

The ministry of thanksgiving

Because the acts of God are the flowing forth of His being, it is difficult to flow forth in gratitude for His being without touching on how His being is manifested. It is difficult to flow forth in gratitude for His character without flowing forth in gratitude for the manifestation of that wonderful character in acts. It is similarly difficult to be carried away in thanksgiving without reference to the Person and character that are seen thus manifested in acts.

Because it is difficult to have praise without thanksgiving and thanksgiving without praise, we shall treat the two together in this book.

There are many ways in which gratitude can be manifested to the Lord for His person and for His deeds. Some of these ways are:

01. By vocal praise and thanksgiving.
02. By costly gifts to the Lord and His service.
03. By a more radical commitment to purity and sanctification.
04. By a more radical surrender to Him, to His will, and to His purposes.
05. By a more radical commitment to His service.
06. By the lifting of the hands in praise.
07. By the clapping of the hands.
08. By song.
09. By a musical instrument.
10. By a joyful noise.

We shall look at these ways of expressing gratitude to God as we go on.

2. GOD'S VALUATION OF PRAISE AND HANKSGIVING

1. IT IS HIS DWELLING PLACE

The Bible says, «Yet thou art holy, enthroned on the praises of Israel» (Psalm 22:3. RSV) .

Yes, the Lord is enthroned on the praises of Israel. He must also be enthroned on the praises of the Church. It must also mean that when a believer begins to praise and thank the Lord, his praises rise and establish a throne for the Lord. It can only be expected that the Lord should come to occupy that throne and, by thus coming, reach out to the praising believer as He would not have done without the praise. So, the praising believer ministers to the Lord in praise and thanksgiving and reaps nearness to God as his own reward!

2. IT IS A WAY OF HONOURING HIM

The Bible says, «He who brings thanksgiving as his sacrifice honours me» (Psalm 50:23 RSV).

A sacrifice of thanksgiving is a way of saying, «I put the Lord first. I put myself last." That is honouring the Lord, is it not?

3. JESUS WANTED IT

The Bible says, «Now on his way to Jerusalem, Jesus travelled along the border between Samaria and Galilee. As he was going into a village, ten men who had leprosy met him. They stood at a distance and called out in a loud voice, 'Jesus, Master, have pity on us!' When he saw them, he said, 'Go, show yourselves to the priests.' As they went, they were cleansed.

One of them, when he saw he was healed, came back, praising God in a loud voice. He threw himself at Jesus' feet and thanked him   and he was a Samaritan.

Jesus asked, 'Were not all ten cleansed? Where are the other nine? Was no one found to return and give praise to God except this foreigner?' Then he said to him, 'Rise and go; your faith has made you well'" (Luke 17:11 19).

These ten lepers had the power to ask. They called out in a loud voice, «Jesus, Master, have pity on us!» There was none of them who did not cry out. All did. The Lord healed them. Nine received their healing and went on their way to enjoy good health. They forgot the Healer. They had time for the healing but they did not care one bit about the Healer. They had used Jesus and that was all. They used Him like a rag and discarded Him, since they did not need Him any more.

One of them came back. He came back praising God in
a loud voice. He was grateful. He was utterly grateful.
He threw himself at Jesus' feet and thanked Him   and he
was a Samaritan. He praised and he thanked. He rendered
the Ministry of Praise and Thanksgiving. He had received
physical healing and came back praising and thanking God.
Because he praised and thanked God, he exposed himself to
the Lord for further ministry. The Lord gave him spiritual
healing. He said to him, «Rise and go, your faith has made
you well.»

He had a spiritual and a physical problem. He saw the
physical problem and cried out to the Lord. The Lord
reached out and met his physical problem. He reached out
and healed him of his physical disease. He came back to
minister to the Lord in praise and thanksgiving; In return
he received from the Lord what he did not ask for   spiritual
healing. That leper, who was a foreigner, received physical
healing and received spiritual healing. He will be in heaven
when Jesus comes for His own. He will resurrect and reign
with the Lord.

Nine of the lepers who received physical healing went away
and never bothered to give thanks. They never came back
to praise the Lord. They never threw themselves at the feet
of Jesus. They never touched Him. They never really knew
Him. They never received spiritual healing. They will not
be in the Kingdom with the Lord Jesus. Their ingratitude

has cost them God's priceless gift of eternal salvation.

The Lord Jesus had wanted to give them physical healing and eternal life. He had decided to do it in stages. They asked for physical healing and He gave them. He had intended that when they each came back to minister to Him in praise and thanksgiving, He would then give them spiritual healing and eternal life. Unfortunately, nine of them were ungrateful and lost out.

When the Lord asked, «Were not all ten cleansed? Where are the other nine? Was no one found to return and give praise to God except this foreigner?» It must have hurt Him deeply, not because they ignored Him, but because of their great loss. It hurt Him that they should have missed the spiritual healing -- the eternal life that He very much wanted to give them. It hurt Him that they had received so little when there was so much to give! It hurt Him that they had lost so much because they would not give so little   praise and thanksgiving -- to Him!!

GOD'S CHAIN BLESSINGS

God's gifts and blessings are a chain. When a person sees his need and asks God to meet it, the Lord does so. Or, if the Lord takes the initiative and moves to bless a man, then the man's need is met. What will happen next depends on the person. If he turns back and comes to the Lord and praises and thanks Him, he will open the door for God to move and do that which the man did not ask for. He will move and do something that is bigger, greater and of more consequence than what was initially received. If he receives the second lot and turns back and invests more time, energy and effort into praising and thanking God, he will open room for God to move in an even greater way in heaping blessings on him. If he continues and grows in the Ministry of Praise and Thanksgiving, he will open himself for more of God's blessings until he overflows with God's blessings.

When he stops praising and thanking God, the additional blessings begin to disappear and, should he not repent and come back to the Ministry of Praise and Thanksgiving, the additional blessings will continue to dwindle until he may finally end up just with what he asked for. We can illustrate what we are saying diagrammatically as follows:

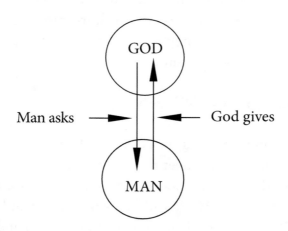

When man asks and God gives, and man receives and goes away, that is the end of the process. The chain has been stopped by the sin of ingratitude.

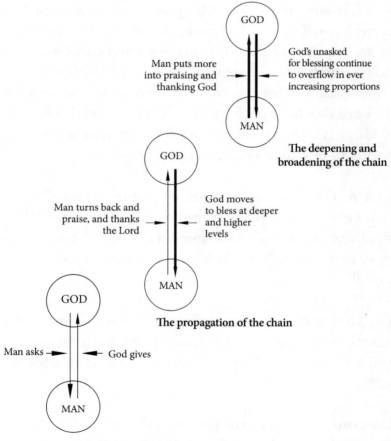

Man puts more into praising and thanking God

God's unasked for blessing continue to overflow in ever increasing proportions

The deepening and broadening of the chain

Man turns back and praise, and thanks the Lord

God moves to bless at deeper and higher levels

The propagation of the chain

Man asks ─ ─ God gives

The beginning of the chain

WHO REALLY BENEFITS FROM PRAISE AND THANKSGIVING ?

We have said that praise and thanksgiving are for the Lord God. They are His portion. This is true. However, as we have just seen, the person who praises and thanks the Lord opens himself for God's greatest blessings. Because this is so, we can also conclude that the one who praises and offers thanksgiving to God is actually sowing seed which will lead to a mighty harvest for him. It is therefore understandable that the Lord should insist that men offer praise and thanksgiving to Him. It is God saying, «Do it for your highest good. Do it so as to reap limitless blessing."

Seen in this light, it becomes even more compelling for each believer to praise and thank the Lord for everything, in all circumstances, at all times and in all places; because by so doing, he is laying hold of God for great blessings for himself.

The Lord said, «Oh, that their hearts would be inclined to fear me and keep all my commands always, so that it might go well with them and their children for ever!» (Deuteronomy 5:29).

The Lord said, «You shall walk in all the way which the Lord your God has commanded you, that you may live, and that it may go well with you, and that you may live long in the land which you shall possess» (Deuteronomy 5:33 RSV).

Moses said to the children of Israel, «And now, O Israel, what does the Lord your God ask of you but to fear the Lord your God, to walk in all his ways, to love him, to serve the Lord your God with all your heart and with all your soul, and to observe the Lord's commands and decrees that I am giving you today for your own good?»(Deuteronomy 10:12 13).

The Lord can do without our praise and thanksgiving. The host of heaven gives Him perfect praise. For example, the Bible says, «Suddenly a great company of the heavenly host appeared with the angel, praising God and saying,

> 'Glory to God in the highest,
> and on earth peace to men
> on whom his favour rests' " (Luke 2:13 14).

The Bible again says, «In the centre, around the throne, were four living creatures, and they were covered with eyes, in front and behind. The first living creature was like a lion, the second was like an ox, the third had a face like a man, the fourth was like a flying eagle. Each of the four living creatures had six wings and was covered with eyes all around, even under his wings. Day and night they never stop saying:

> 'Holy, holy, holy,
> is the Lord God Almighty,

who was, and is, and is to come.'

Whenever the living creatures give glory, honour and thanks to him who sits on the throne and who lives for ever and ever, the twenty four elders fall down before him who sits on the throne, and worship him who lives for ever and ever. They lay their crowns before the throne and say:

> 'You are worthy, our Lord and God,
> to receive glory and honour and power,
> for you created all things,
> and by your will they were created
> and have their being' " (Revelation 4:6 11).

So the Lord can do without our praise. He is not short of praise. He is being praised unceasingly in His immediate presence. He has ordained praise and thanksgiving for our good. We praise Him for our good. We praise Him in all circumstances, for everything, at all times for our good. If we do not praise Him, we lose. He loses nothing.

Let us praise Him unceasingly.

Hallelujah ! Amen.

03. GIVING THANKS WHEN THINGS GO THE WAY THAT IS OBVIOUSLY A BLESSING TO US

There are many things in our lives in which God has intervened miraculously, which can be called the special events of our lives. That is where we ought to begin to carry out the Ministry of Praise and Thanksgiving. Some time ago I wrote down some such events in my life; so that I could give thanks specially to the Lord. I will put out my own list for you to see and then you can follow suit for your life.

1. An exceptional father.
2. An exceptional mother.
3. An elder brother radically committed to my academic success.
4. An unusual environment for the first four years of my Primary School life.
5. Being first in class at the end of the first year in Primary School.
6. Mr Esombe, my teacher in the second year in Primary School, who loved me exceptionally and caused me to study unusually.
7. Lambert Eteng Ebot who became my friend in the second year in Primary School.
8. An exceptional performance at the end of the second year in Primary School with 598 marks out of a total of

600. The two marks were lost because I gave the names of ten of the disciples of the Lord Jesus instead of twelve.

9. A price of three pence won during the second year in Primary School for being able to answer Arithmetic questions that some boys in the 6th year could not answer.

10. Two shillings earned for working on one man's coffee farm every week for eight weeks without anyone noticing my absence from home, and the joy of being congratulated and carried shoulder high by my darling father when I gave him the money and told him how I had earned it.

11. That day in 1955, at the age of ten, when my darling father gave me that evangelistic tract, «Someone Died For You,» and I understood for the first time that the Lord Jesus died for me as an individual, and thus I was led to invite Him to come into my heart as my Lord and Saviour.

12. That same day in 1955 when, after I received the Lord Jesus, I ran without stopping to the next village which was two kilometres away in order to tell my friend Reuben Unota Mbah that Someone died for him. (He did not understand. I was too excited and too full of joy because of my discovery to have explained things clearly to him).

13. December 1955 when I was the general second in a competitive examination for all the Schools in Ngie, even though I had changed schools from Nyasoso to Andek,

Ngie that June.

14. 1957 when my darling father made me his friend following my demonstration of unusual financial responsibility.

15. 1959 when I passed the entrance examination into Cameroon Protestant College, Bali.

16. 16th January 1960 when I went to Secondary School.

17. April 1960 when I won a government scholarship for secondary education through success in the scholarship examination. Without this scholarship, it would have been impossible for me to continue with secondary education, as my pastor father did not have the funds that could see me through Secondary School.

18. February 1960 when I was introduced to the group that went out on Sundays for evangelism by John Gwan. I went out with him and others for evangelism in the villages of Bali. This was a most serious step; for it introduced me into the group of spiritually minded students. It was a step that had profound effects on my spiritual life in every way.

19. 1962 when I met a girl called Agnes. She said I was a king; that I was her king. Those words made me believe myself. They also made me determine that I would never do anything that was not worthy of a king.

20. 1962 when I was second as the junior librarian of Cameroon Protestant College.

21. 1963 when I was elected prefect in charge of the library, evening studies and information in the college. This

was a serious step because it brought heavy leadership responsibilities upon me.

22. 1963 when I was elected President of the Moghamo Students' Association.

23. 1963 when I was elected Secretary General of the North West Students' Association.

24. 1964 when I passed the entrance examination into Cameroon College of Arts, Science and Technology. I was the 13th by order of merit of the nearly 100 students who were admitted. The miracle of God in it was that the first 13 students were given Federal Government Scholarships of 30.000 francs per year plus other privileges. The year before, the first ten were given Federal Scholarships, but the Scholarship Board chose to give 13 Scholarships in my year because I was the 13th! The year that followed, no Federal Scholarships were given!

25. 1964 when a girl on the Campus in Bambili came to me and said, «Is it because you are handsome that you snob all the girls and would not talk to any?» This comment encouraged me to accept myself because, with slightly curved legs, I thought I was considered ugly. In fact, I used to pray and ask God to make my legs straight. Because they were not straight, I thought I was ugly. So this girl's complement had healing and assuring influence on me.

26. December 21st 1964 when I met Prisca ...

27. January 26th 1965 when I received the first letter from

Prisca.

28. April 1965 when there was an accident on the Bambili Bamenda road. A woman died in it. A number of us saw the corpse and vowed that we would never sin again; that we would walk with God and prepare for heaven.

29. April 1966 when I was admitted into Fourah Bay College, Sierra Leone, to do a degree course in Science.

30. April 1966 when I was selected by the Cameroon government for a Canadian scholarship to study medicine in Canada. Everything was set for the trip medical examination, and all else. I did not go because the General Certificate of Education, Advanced Level, results for Cameroon came from London one week too late for me to go to Canada for that year. I was asked to wait for one year. I did not wait to go to Canada the next year. I left for Sierra Leone on September 27th 1966, to study for a Bachelor of Science degree.

31. 1st October 1966 when I met the Lord Jesus and my life was transformed. I gave Him my heart and my life and promised to serve Him with all my spirit, soul and body. I also made it my goal to labour to ensure that all Africa is saved from the colonialism of sin and the neocolonialism of self.

I will stop my list here at my encounter with the Lord Jesus and my surrender and consecration to Him, so that you too may begin to work on the list of the important positive events of your life. My list goes up to 250 events, right up to December 1991. Work on a similar list for your life and, perhaps for the first time in your life, set aside a ten day Season of Praise and Thanksgiving for God's interventions in your life. Set aside one hour per day for praise and thanksgiving. On day one, praise and thank the Lord for the first twenty five events on your list. On day two, praise and thank the Lord for the next twenty five events, and then go on in that same way day by day until day ten when you will praise and give thanks to the Lord for the last twenty five events that you wrote down.

You may find that you were able to write down five hundred special events in your life. That is wonderful. You can then make your Special Season of Praise and Thanksgiving to last for twenty days. If you have one thousand special events, then you can have your Special Season of Praise and Thanksgiving for 40 days. In fact, a Special Season of Praise and Thanksgiving of forty days will flow to the Lord as a sweet smelling offering. It will bless His all holy and His all blessed name. It will also leave great marks on your life.

In order to help you to see and write out the great interventions of God in your life, or the high moments or special events of your life, perhaps you can regroup them as follows:

1. The great events of my physical life.
2. Great events in my relationships with people of the opposite sex.

3. Great events in my friendship with people of my sex.
4. Great events in my relationship with my father.
5. Great events in my relationship with my mother.
6. Great events in my relationship with my brothers and sisters.
7. Great events in my academic life.
8. Great events in my relationship with sicknesses and diseases.
9. Great events in my relationship with strangers.
10. Great events in my relationship with my friend and friends.
11. Great events in my relationship with my co workers.
12. Great events in my relationship with my wife or husband.
13. Great events in my relationship with our children.
14. Great events in my prayer life.
15. Great events in my giving to the Lord.
16. Great events in my fasting life.
17. Great events in my life as an evangelist.
18. Great events in my life as a soul winner.
19. Great events in my life as a Bible Teacher.
20. Great events in my life as a pastor.
21. Great events in my life as a writer for God.
22. Great events in my life as a seeker after God.
23. Great events in my studies in the School of Knowing God.
24. Great events in my studies in the School of Dying to Self.
25. Great events in my studies in the School of Being a Servant of All.

26. Great events in my studies in the School of Leading God's people.
27. Great events in my financial life.
28. Great events in my professional life.
29. Great events in my relationship with my enemies and adversaries.
30. Great events in my reading of the Bible.
31. Great events in my listening to the Gospel preached.

You can see that if you are able to write ten events in each section, you will easily have three hundred topics for your first Special Season of Praise and Thanksgiving. You may find that you do not have many things to write out and praise the Lord for under a particular heading. You will find, on the other hand, that you have very many under another heading. Certainly, you can easily find material for your first Special Season of Praise and Thanksgiving.

Do not be put off by the words «great events.» You may call them significant events. These will include things that happened to you distinctly and that make you say in your heart, «Thanks be to the Lord for allowing these things to happen to me. I was highly blessed by them.»

You may find that you do not remember things clearly. Man has an unusual capacity to forget things that happened and were special blessings at the time they happened. At that moment they brought special relief, special joy and special thanksgiving to the Lord. God did indeed intervene.

Afterwards, as the days went by and other pressures came in, that special event which was so special becomes increasingly ordinary until finally it is as if nothing happened at all. Take the following as examples and you will see clearly what I am saying:

1. Your attitude to the girl you married on the day you proposed to her and she said, «Yes,» and your attitude to her six months afterwards as you prepared for the wedding.

2. Your attitude to your wife on the day you wedded and your appreciation of your wedding day ten years afterwards.

3. Your joy of salvation on the day you received the Lord and your joy of salvation six years afterwards.

4. Your joy in speaking in other tongues the day you received that gift and your joy about the reception of the gift two years after you have been using it.

5. The joy of receiving a gift at the moment of receiving the gift and your attitude and estimation of it many months afterwards.

Because we are apt to minimize events when we look at them in retrospect, forgetting how important they were to us soon after they happened, it is good to record the great events of our lives as soon as they happen. In that way, we shall be able to continue to give praise and thanksgiving to the Lord for them long after they have happened.

PRAISE AND THANKSGIVING APPRECIATE GOD'S DEEDS

When a person singles out the interventions of God in his life and gives thanks for them, he appreciates the events and gives them importance. As he praises and thanks the Lord repeatedly for the same event, the event becomes increasingly more significant until it is valued by man as God values it.

When a person does not single out an event for special praise and thanksgiving to the Lord, he depreciates the event so that it has decreasing value, and finally it is as if God did not do anything at all.

It is bad to depreciate the acts of God. This is done by forgetting what He did. It is also done by remembering them and failing to thank the Lord for them. This shortens God's hand and stands in the way of His doing more. One way to ensure that events are not forgotten is to record them.

04. GOD IS INTERESTED IN ACCURATE RECORDS

Our God is interested in records. He is interested in accurate records: Look at the following passage of the Bible:

«Here are the stages in the journey of the Israelites when they came out of Egypt by divisions under the leadership of Moses and Aaron. At the Lord's command Moses recorded the stages in their journey. This is their journey by stages:

The Israelites set out from Rameses on the fifteenth day of the first month, the day after the Passover. They matched out boldly in full view of all the Egyptians, who were burying all their firstborn, whom the Lord had stricken down among them; for the Lord had brought judgment on their gods.
The Israelites left Rameses and camped at Succoth.
They left Succoth and camped at Etham, on the edge of the desert.

They left Etham, turned back to Pi Hahiroth, to the east of Baal Zephon, and camped near Migdol.
They left Pi Hahiroth and passed through the sea into the desert, and when they had travelled for three days in the Desert of Etham, they camped at Marah.
They left Marah and went to Elim, where there were twelve springs and seventy palm trees, and they camped there.
They left Elim and camped by the Red Sea.
They left the Red Sea and camped in the Desert of Sin.

They left the Desert of Sin and camped at Dophkah.
They left Dophkah and camped at Alush.

They left Alush and camped at Rephidim, where there was
no water for the people to drink.
They left Rephidim and camped in the Desert of Sinai.
They left the Desert of Sinai and camped at Kibroth
Hattaavah.
They left Kibroth Hattaavah and camped at Hazeroth.
They left Hazeroth and camped at Rithmah.
They left Rithmah and camped at Rimmon Perez.
They left Rimmon Perez and camped at Libnah.
They left Libnah and camped at Rissah.
They left Rissah and camped at Kehelathah.
They left Kehelathah and camped at Mount Shepher.
They left Mount Shepher and camped at Haradah.
They left Haradah and camped at Makheloth.
They left Makheloth and camped at Tahath.
They left Tahath and camped at Terah.
They left Terah and camped at Mithcah.
They left Mithcah and camped at Hashmonah.
They left Hashmonah and camped at Moseroth.
They left Moseroth and camped at Bene Jaakan.
They left Bene Jaakan and camped at Hor Haggidgad.
They left Hor Haggidgad and camped at Jotbathah.
They left Jotbathah and camped at Abronah.
They left Abronah and camped at Ezion Geber.
They left Ezion Geber and camped at Kadesh, in the Desert
of Zin.

They left Kadesh and camped at Mount Hor, on the border of Edom. At the Lord's command Aaron the priest went up Mount Hor, where he died on the first day of the first month of the fortieth year after the Israelites came out of Egypt. Aaron was a hundred and twenty three years old when he died on Mount Hor. The Canaanite King of the Arabs, who lived in the Negeb of Canaan, heard that the Israelites were coming.

They left Mount Hor and camped at Zalmonah.

They left Zalmonah and camped at Punon.

They left Punon and camped at Oboth.

They left Oboth and camped at Iye Abarim, on the boarder of Moab.

They left Iye and camped at Dibon Gad.

They left Dibon Gad and camped at Almon Diblathaim.

They left Almon Diblathaim and camped in the mountains of Abarim, near Nebo.

They left the mountains of Abarim and camped on the plains of Moab by the Jordan across from Jericho. There on the plains of Moab they camped along the Jordan from Beth Jeshimoth to Abel Shittim.

On the plains of Moab by the Jordan across from Jericho the Lord said to Moses, 'Speak to the Israelites and say to them: 'When you cross the Jordan into Canaan, drive out all the inhabitants of the land before you. Destroy all their carved images and their cast idols, and demolish all their high places. Take possession of the land and settle in it, for I have given the land to you to possess. Distribute the land by lot, according to your clans. To a larger group give a larger inheritance, and to a smaller group a smaller one. Whatever falls to them by lot will be theirs. Distribute it according to your ancestral tribes.

'But if you do not drive out the inhabitants of the land, those you allow to remain will become barbs in your eyes and thorns in your sides. They will give you trouble in the land where you will live. And then I will do to you what I plan to do to them'" (Numbers 33:1 56).

It is quite obvious that the Lord is interested in details. Let us look at some examples in the passage before us:

1. He did not just say that the Israelites left Egypt. He commanded it to be written that they set out from Rameses on the fifteenth day of the first month, the day after the Passover.

2. He got it recorded that they matched out boldly in full view of all the Egyptians.

3. He got it recorded that the Egyptians were burying their dead firstborn when the Israelites were marching out.

4. He got it recorded how the death of the firstborn had come about.

5. He had it recorded that at Elim there were twelve springs and seventy palm trees.

Why did the Lord go into these details? There are many possible reasons for it. The first one is that it is consistent with His character. He is a God of exactitude. He is a God of details. He numbers the hair of the human head and none can fall off without His knowing and without His permission. He records each word you speak, and so on. He is a God of accuracy and exactitude. Another reason why He got the details recorded is so that that generation and the succeeding generations might praise and thank Him for what He did. He is interested in detailed praise; and for detailed praise to come to Him, the details of His deeds have to be recorded, so that praise should come to Him with each detail.

I have had to stop and bless the Lord for each of the twelve springs that He provided at Elim for the supply of water for His children. I have had to stop and thank the Lord for each of the seventy palm trees which were at Elim, and for the shelter that each gave to some of God's children. I have had to thank and praise the Lord for each stage in the journey from Egypt to Canaan, thanking Him for having made all of it possible, thanking Him for the impact of that journey and the Israeli settlement in Canaan, the history of the salvation of the world through the blood of the Lord Jesus, and for my own salvation that cannot be dissociated from Israeli settlement in Canaan.

How would such praise have been possible had the Lord not caused the details to be written?

5. DAILY CALENDAR OF PRAISE AND THANKSGIVING

You should set fifteen minutes aside each day for routine praise and thanksgiving. The following items could be included in the items of praise and thanksgiving.

1. For God's holiness that cannot be compromised.
2. For God's great glory that fills the entire universe.
3. For God's unusual capacity to love the most undeserving.
4. For God's unchanging faithfulness.
5. For God's mighty power that cannot be resisted.
6. For God's immense kindness to the sons of men in general and to you in particular.
7. For God's word that will never pass away.
8. For God's sovereignty in creation, salvation, and in all else.
9. For the Lord Jesus Christ, the Wonderful Counsellor, Mighty God, Prince of Peace.
10. For the Lord's incarnation.
11. For the Lord's humiliation.
12. For the Lord's death on the Cross.
13. For the Lord's resurrection.
14. For the Lord's enthronement.
15. For the Lord's intercession from the throne.
16. For the Holy Spirit whom the Lord Jesus received from the Father and sent into the world.
17. For the Pentecost.

18. For the day the Holy Spirit brought you to Jesus.
19. For your personal «Pentecost.»
20. For the Holy Spirit's work as Counsellor.
21. For the Holy Spirit's work as Comforter.
22. For the Holy Spirit's work as Guide.
23. For the Holy Spirit's work as Teacher.
24. For the Holy Spirit as the One who produces the character of Christ in the believer.
25. For the Holy Spirit as One who gives gifts to the Church and to individuals.
26. For the Holy Spirit as the Sanctifier.
27. For the Body of believers.
28. For your conscience.
29. For your intuition.
30. For your communion.
31. For your will.
32. For your mind.
33. For your emotions.
34. For your blood.
35. For your bones.
36. For your muscles.
37. For your capacity to see spiritually.
38. For your capacity to see physically.
39. For your parents and ancestors.
40. For your partner.
41. For your children.
42. For your relatives.
43. For your friend.
44. For your friends.

45. For those you love.
46. For those who love you.
47. For your job.
48. For your income.
49. For God's goodness to you yesterday.
50. For God's goodness to you today.
51. For God's goodness to you in the future.
52. For your sin which God covered.
53. For your sin which God convicted you of and you repented.
54. For your sin which God exposed to others.
55. For your beautiful or handsome appearance.
56. For your capacity to speak.
57. For your capacity to understand.
58. For your capacity to smell.
59. For your capacity to feel.
60. For your desire for holiness.
61. For practical steps you took recently to terminate with sin.
62. For the sin that held you captive in the past but now you have been totally set free from it.
63. For the person you presented the gospel to recently.
64. For the ministry that the Lord has given you.
65. For the opportunity which God has given you to be a servant to another.
66. For the food that you will eat today.
67. For the food that you ate yesterday.
68. For the food that you will eat tomorrow.
69. For the protection that the Lord granted you while you slept.

70. For the time you spent in prayer yesterday.
71. For the time you have spent, or will spend in prayer today.
72. For the time you will spend in prayer tomorrow.
73. For the time you spent reading the Bible yesterday.
74. For the time you will spend or you have spent reading the Bible today
75. For the time you will spend reading the Bible tomorrow.
76. For the time you spent meeting God yesterday.
77. For the time you will spend or you have spent meeting God today.
78. For the time you will spend meeting God tomorrow.
79. For your financial needs which God provided yesterday.
80. For your financial needs which God will provide today.
81. For your financial needs which God will provide tomorrow.
82. For the good works that God planned for you to do today.
83. For the person whom God sent your way yesterday and from whom you learnt something new about the Lord, about yourself or about the world.
84. For the person whom God will send your way today to teach you something new.
85. For the person whom God will send your way tomorrow to teach you something new.
86. For the water that is available for you to drink.
87. For the air that the Lord has given you to breathe.
88. For the pleasant surprise that God has in store for you today.

89. For the strength that the Lord will give you today to do all of His will.
90. For the capacity to see God's goodness in your life today.
91. For the capacity to see God's goodness in others today.
92. For a spirit of obedience to Him and to His word that He has given you.
93. For a spirit of submission to His will that He has given you.
94. For the opportunity you had yesterday to give yourself away in order to meet someone's need.
95. For the opportunity you will have today to give yourself away so that someone's need should be met.
96. For the opportunity you will have tomorrow to give yourself away so that someone's need should be met.
97. For your growing capacity to love the Lord.
98. For your capacity to say, 'No,' to the flesh.
99. For your growing capacity to desire the Lord and to desire His return.

6. THE POWER OF COLD ROUTINE

There was a song that some sang thus:, «Every time I feel the Spirit moving in my heart I will pray; every time I feel the Spirit moving in my heart I will pray.»

It is good to pray when one feels the Spirit moving. Such prayer goes to the Lord and He receives it and answers. However, the person who only prays when he feels the Spirit moving in his heart is being led, not by the Word of God nor by the Spirit, but by his feelings. Such a person could enter into a period when, for days upon days, he may not pray because he has not felt the Spirit moving. He could become an easy prey to the enemy.

To avoid this condition, a man should settle it in his heart that he will praise and thank the Lord whether or not he feels like it.

It is best to establish a routine programme of praise. Why not set a fixed hour of each day for praise and thanksgiving, regardless of how you feel? That programme could run as follows:

Saturday : Praise and Thanksgiving for what God did in your life last week.

Sunday : Praise and Thanksgiving for what God did in your family last week.

Monday : Praise and Thanksgiving for what God did in your neighbourhood last week.

Tuesday : Praise and Thanksgiving for what God did in your city last week.

Wednesday : Praise and Thanksgiving for what God did in your nation last week.

Thursday : Praise and Thanksgiving for what God did in your continent last week.

Friday : Praise and Thanksgiving for what God did on Planet Earth last week.

You may decide that this praise and thanksgiving time will be between 9 p.m. and 10 p.m. Well, that is your decision. However, after you have chosen the hour, consecrate it to the Lord and covenant with Him that you shall be there to bring Him the praise and thanksgiving that He deserves and, may I dare to say, the praise and thanksgiving that He needs!

You will find that it is sometimes just cold routine. However, cold routine is powerful and indispensable. Think about the cold routine of breathing in and breathing out. There are no joyous feelings accompanying it, but what if that routine were to stop? The consequences you know. Another cold routine is that of the heart pumping blood to various parts of the body. What happens when that routine stops? Think of the routine of the earth's rotation. What would happen if it stopped?

If you think about it carefully, you will find that life is dependent more on routine acts than on occasional events, important as these may be. Great things are accomplished by routine. More is accomplished by routine than by special events.

I suggest to you that if something is really important, convert it into a routine activity and your success is guaranteed. Prayer is important. Establish it as a routine and ignore your feelings. Work and walk by your established programme and not by sudden exciting happenings that soon pass away. Decide, for example, that you will pray for each of the eight watches of the day and night. Decide that you will pray at every watch for 15 minutes. This will mean praying for 15 minutes at:

1. Midnight.
2. Three o'clock in the morning.
3. Six o'clock in the morning.
4. Nine o'clock in the morning.
5. Midday.
6. Three o'clock in the afternoon.
7. Six o'clock in the evening.
8. Nine o'clock at night.

If you follow this routine, you will be praying for 120 minutes every 24 hours. This will raise you to one of the praying people of our generation, and you will have a standing with God.

If you follow the routine for long enough, your entire body will adapt to it and you will find it easy to wake up at each watch and find it easy to go back to sleep.

Actually, God did not give man a body so that that body should hinder him from spiritual progress. The body is not an enemy. The body is a servant to be tamed and used at will. However, you must tame and educate it to do what you want!

So, decide on one hour of praise and thanksgiving every day and follow a routine programme. Supplement your routine programme with thanksgiving at all the other times when excitement leads you to praise and thanksgiving.

GROWING IN ROUTINE PRAISE AND THANKSGIVING

You may not know God enough to be able to spend one hour in His presence in praise and thanksgiving. Do not give up because of that. You should begin where you are in your relationship with Him.

It is not too small to begin with one minute of praise and thanksgiving daily. Do this faithfully for one month until you find that your being has begun to look up to that one minute. You can then move to two minutes a day,

- five minutes,
- ten minutes,
- fifteen minutes,
- twenty minutes,
- thirty minutes,
- forty five minutes,
- one hour a day.

It is important that you understand that the amount of time that you are able to spend in God's presence in praise and thanksgiving is determined, not only by the availability of things to praise and thank the Lord for, but also by your God content. If you know God only a little, you will not be able to spend long periods in praise and thanksgiving, even if you want to. But as you grow to know Him and to love Him increasingly, you will find that one hour may not be enough to thank the Lord for what happened in your life or in your family in the past week.

Be honest and true.

Also determine to make progress.

You may be able to set the goal of being able to spend one

hour daily in praise and thanksgiving in the next twelve months. You can then start with one minute or five minutes in Week One of the first month and then grow as the Lord enables you. If you labour to spend five minutes in praise every day during the first month, you may be able to move on to ten minutes during the second month and so on until your goal is attained.

Because there are many blessings associated with praise and thanksgiving to the Lord, the one who disciplines himself and enrols in the «School of Praise and Thanksgiving» will find that withdrawal from that School is most unlikely. If he stays there long enough, he will become «addicted» to Praise and Thanksgiving. He will also become «addicted» to purity of heart; for only the pure in heart can sustain the light that shines from the God who is praised. So the routine of praise and thanksgiving will slowly but steadily transform the person into a mature worshipper of the Lord.

It will also transform him into a God conscious person. When a man has to ask daily, «What is God doing in

- my life,
- my family,
- my quarter or neighbourhood,
- my city,
- my nation,
- my continent,
- my planet ?»

he is asking, «How Is The Holy Spirit Moving In My Day?» He will be open. He will gather the facts. He will be filled with evidence that God is at work in His universe. He will grow in faith and love and all else. He will love routine praise and, before long, he will realize that cold praise has been transformed into hot praise. Hallelujah ! Amen.

7. A SONG UNTO THE LORD IN THE HOUR OF VICTORY

It is normal for there to be a spontaneous Song of Praise and Thanksgiving to the Lord in the moment of victory. When the Lord brings sudden deliverance or does an unexpected thing that blesses, spontaneous songs of praise ought to flow to Him as a way of expressing gratitude. In addition to these, it is normal for Spirit filled people to flow forth in praise and thanksgiving. When people walk with God, they tend to break forth into songs of praise with every fresh encounter with God. It is as if when God touches man afresh with blessing, the response is praise and thanksgiving, often in words of prayer, but also in song a Song of Praise and Thanksgiving.

A Song of Praise and Thanksgiving does not always need to be spontaneous. It could be the fruit of cold calculations and a calm working at it for hours, days and weeks until it is all ready. Small portions of it may be sung to the Lord as they are ready, but the one who wants to bring a special song of praise and thanksgiving to the Lord may keep working at it, changing parts and adding others. He will labour at it until it is the best that can be offered to the Lord. Then he will sing it to the Lord. He may keep it to sing it over and over to the Lord. He may teach others to sing it to the Lord. He will ensure that praise goes to the Lord by song. Amen.

A SONG UNTO THE LORD IN THE HOUR OF VICTORY

1. THE SONG OF MOSES AND ISRAEL AT THE RED SEA

When the Lord delivered Israel at the Red Sea and drowned the Egyptians, Moses and Israel sang the following song of spontaneous praise to the Lord:

> «I will sing to the Lord, for he is highly exalted.
> The horse and its rider he has hurled into the sea.
> The Lord is my strength and my song; he has become my salvation.
> He is my God, and I will praise him, my father's God, and I will exalt him.
> The Lord is a warrior; the Lord is his name.
> Pharaoh's chariots and his army he has hurled into the sea.
> The best of Pharaoh's officers are drowned in the

Red Sea.
The deep waters have covered them; they sank to the
depth like a stone.
«Your right hand, O Lord, was majestic in power.
Your right hand, O Lord, shattered the enemy.
In the greatness of your majesty you threw down
those who opposed you.
You unleashed your burning anger; it consumed
them like stubble.
By the blast of your nostrils the waters piled up.
The surging waters stood firm like a wall; the deep
waters congealed in the heart of the sea.
«The enemy boasted, 'I will pursue, I will overtake
them.
I will divide the spoils; I will gorge myself on them.
I will draw my sword and my hand will destroy them.'
But you blew with your breath, and the sea
covered them.
They sank like lead in the mighty waters.
«Who among the gods is like you, O Lord? Who is
like you majestic in holiness, awesome in glory
working wonders?
You stretched out your right hand and the earth
 swallowed them.
«In your unfailing love you will lead the people you
have redeemed.
In your strength you will guide them to your holy
dwelling.
The nations will hear and tremble; anguish will grip

the people of Philistia.
The chiefs of Edom will be terrified, the leaders of
Moab will be seized with trembling, the people of
Canaan will melt away; terror and dread will fall
upon them.
By the power of your arm they will be as still as a
stone   until your people pass by, O Lord, until the
people you bought pass by.
You will bring them in and plant them on the
mountain of your inheritance   the place, O Lord,
you made for your dwelling, the sanctuary, O Lord,
your hands established.
The Lord will reign for ever and ever»
(Exodus 15:1 18).

In this Song of Praise and Thanksgiving at the moment of
great victory, Moses and Israel did not just throw empty
words at the Lord. In the song, praise is given to the Lord
for what He did, who He was in the past, who He is in the
present and for what He will do in the future. The song
shows clearly that the facts of what God did were known
clearly and the facts of what God would do in the future
were also clearly known. Moses and Israel knew who future
enemies were likely to be   Philistia, Edom, Moab and
Canaan, and they praised the Lord in anticipation,

«The chiefs of Edom will be terrified,
the leaders of Moab will be seized with trembling,

the people of Canaan will melt away;
terror and dread will fall upon them.
By the power of your arm they will be as still
      as stone   until your people pass by, until the
      people you bought pass by ...»

The song flowed from a deep knowledge of God. Obviously,
Moses must have composed the song and Israel sang it after
him. That is where the depth of his knowledge of the Lord
came through.

2. THE SONG OF DEBORAH AND BARAK ON THE DEFEAT OF JABIN

When Deborah and Barak went to war against Jabin, a king
of Canaan who reigned in Hazor, the Lord subdued Jabin
before Israel. The hand of the Israelites grew stronger
and stronger against Jabin, the Canaanite king, until they
destroyed him. On that day, Deborah and Barak son of
Abinoam sang this song:

    «When the princes in Israel take the lead,
    when the people willingly offer themselves
    praise the Lord!
    «Hear this, you kings! Listen, you rulers!
    I will sing to the Lord, I will sing;
    I will make music to the Lord, the God of Israel.

«O Lord, when you went out from Seir,
when you marched from the land of Edom,

the earth shook, the heavens poured, the clouds
poured down water.

The mountains quaked before the Lord, the One of
Sinai, before the Lord, the God of Israel.

«In the days of Shamgar son of Anath,
in the days of Joel, the roads abandoned;
travellers took to winding paths.
Village life in Israel ceased, ceased until I, Deborah
arose, arose a mother in Israel.
When they chose new gods, war came to the city
gates, and not a shield or spear was seen among the
forty thousand in Israel.
My heart is with Israel's princes, with the willing
volunteers among the people.
Praise the Lord!

"You who ride on white donkeys, sitting on your
saddle blankets, and you who walk along the road,
consider the voice of the singers at the watering
places, They recite the righteous acts of the Lord,
the righteous acts of his warriors in Israel.

«Then the people of the Lord went down to the city
gates.
'Wake up, wake up, Deborah!
Wake up, wake up, break out in song!

Arise, O Barak!
Take captive your captives, O son of Abinoam.'

«Then the men who were left came down to the
 nobles;
the people of the Lord came to me with the mighty.
Some came from Ephraim, whose roots were in
Amalek;
Benjamin was with the people who followed you.

From Makir captains came down, from Zebulun
those who bear a commander's staff.
The Princes of Issachar were with Deborah; yes,
Issachar was with Barak, rushing after him into the
valley; In the districts of Reuben there was much
searching of heart.
Why did you stay among the campfires to hear the
whistling of the flocks?
In the districts of Reuben there was much searching
of heart.
Gilead stayed beyond the Jordan.
And Dan, why did you linger by the ships?
Asher remained on the coast and stayed in his coves.
The people of Zebulun risked their very lives; so did
Naphthali on the heights of the field.

«Kings came, they fought; the kings of Canaan
fought at Taanach by the waters of Megiddo, but
they carried off no silver, no plunder.
From the heavens the stars fought, from their courses

they fought against Sisera.
The river Kishon swept them away, the age old river,
the river Kishon.
March on, my soul; be strong!
Then thundered the horses' hoofs -- galloping,
galloping go his mighty steeds.
'Curse Meroz,' said the angel of the Lord.
'Curse its people bitterly, because they did not come
to help the Lord, to help the Lord against the mighty.'

«Most blessed of women be Jael, the wife of Heber
the Kenite, most blessed of tent dwelling women.
He asked for water, and she gave him milk;
in a bowl fit for nobles she brought him curdled milk.
Her hand reached for the tent peg, her right hand for
the workman's hammer.

She struck Sisera, she crushed his head, she shattered
and pierced his temple.
At her feet he sank, he fell; there he lay.
At her feet he sank, he fell; where he sank, there he
fell -- dead.

«Through the window peered Sisera's mother; behind
the lattice she cried out,
'Why is his chariot so long in coming? Why is the
 clatter of his chariots delayed?'
The wisest of her ladies answered her; indeed, she
keeps saying to herself,

'Are they not finding and dividing the spoils; a girl or
two for each man,
colourful garments as plunder for Sisera,
colourful garments embroidered,
highly embroidered garments for my neck -- all this
as plunder?'

«So may all your enemies perish, O Lord!
But may they who love you be like the sun when it
rises in its strength»

(Judges 5:1 31).

3. HANNAH'S PRAYER AT THE DEDICATION OF SAMUEL

Then Hannah prayed and said:

«My heart rejoices in the Lord;
in the Lord my horn is lifted high.
My mouth boasts over my enemies,
for I delight in thy deliverance.

«There is no-one holy like the Lord;
there is no-one besides you;
there is no Rock like our God.

«Do not keep talking so proudly

or let your mouth speak such arrogance,
for the Lord is a God who knows,
and by him deeds are weighed.

«The bows of the warriors are broken,
but those who stumbled are armed with strength.
Those who were full hire themselves out for food,
but those who were hungry hunger no more.
She who was barren has borne seven children,
but she who has had many sons pines away.

"The Lord brings death and makes alive;
he brings down to the grave and raises up.
The Lord sends poverty and wealth;
he humbles and he exalts.
He raises the poor from the dust
and lifts the needy from the ash heap;
he seats them with princes
and has them inherit a throne of honour.

«For the foundations of the earth are the Lord's;
upon them he has set the world.
He will guard the feet of his saints,
but the wicked will be silenced in darkness.

«It is not by strength that one prevails;
those who oppose the Lord will be shattered.
He will thunder against them from heaven;
the Lord will judge the ends of the earth.

«He will give strength to his king
and exalt the horn of his anointed»
(1 Samuel 2:1 10).

4. MARY'S SONG OF PRAISE AND THANKSGIVING UPON REALISATION THAT SHE WAS PREGNANT WITH THE LORD JESUS.

"The angel Gabriel told Mary, 'Do not be afraid, Mary, you have found favour with God. You will be with child and give birth to a son, and you are to give him the name Jesus. He will be great and will be called the Son of the Most High. The Lord God will give him the throne of his father David, and he will reign over the house of Jacob for ever; his kingdom will never end.'

'How will this be,' Mary asked the angel, 'since I am a virgin?'

The angel answered, 'The Holy Spirit will come upon you, and the power of the Most High will overshadow you. So the holy one to be born will be called the Son of God. Even Elizabeth your relative is going to have a child in her old age, and she who was said to be barren is in her sixth month. For nothing is impossible with God.'

'I am the Lord's servant,' Mary answered. 'May it be to me

as you have said.' Then the angel left her.

At that time Mary got ready and hurried to a town in the hill country of Judea, where she entered Zechariah's home and greeted Elizabeth. When Elizabeth heard Mary's greetings, the baby leaped in her womb, and Elizabeth was filled with the Holy Spirit. In a loud voice she exclaimed: 'Blessed are you among women, and blessed is the child you will bear! But why am I so favoured, that the mother of my Lord should come to me? As soon as the sound of your greeting reached my ears, the baby in my womb leaped for joy. Blessed is she who has believed that what the Lord has said to her will be accomplished!'

And Mary said:

> 'My soul glorifies the Lord
> and my spirit rejoices in God my Saviour,
> for he has been mindful
> of the humble state of his servant.
> From now on all generations will call me blessed,
> for the Mighty One has done great things for me
> holy is his name.
> His mercy extends to those who fear him,
> from generation to generation.
> He has performed mighty deeds with his arm;
> he has scattered those who are proud in their inmost
> thoughts.
> He has brought down rulers from their thrones

but has lifted up the humble.
He has filled the hungry with good things
but has sent the rich away empty.
He has helped his servant Israel,
remembering to be merciful
to Abraham and his descendants forever,
even as he said to our fathers' "

(Luke 1:29 55).

5. ZECHARIAH'S PROPHECY OF PRAISE AND THANKSGIVING AT THE BIRTH OF JOHN AND THE OPENING OF HIS MOUTH AND LOOSING OF HIS TONGUE

«When it was time for Elizabeth to have her baby, she gave birth to a son. Her neighbours and relatives heard that the Lord had shown her great mercy, and they shared her joy.

On the eighth day they came to circumcise the child, and they were going to name him after his father Zechariah, but his mother spoke up and said, 'No! He is to be called John.' They said to her, 'There is no-one among your relatives who has that name.' Then they made signs to his father, to find out what he would like to name the child. He asked for a writing tablet, and to everyone's astonishment he wrote, 'His name is John.' Immediately his mouth was opened and his tongue was loosed, and he began to speak, praising God. The neighbours were all filled with awe, and throughout the hill country of Judea people were talking about all these things. Everyone who heard this wondered about it, asking, 'What then is this child going to be?' For the Lord's hand was with him.

His father Zechariah was filled with the Holy Spirit and prophesied:

> 'Praise be to the Lord, the God of Israel,
> because he has come and has redeemed his people.
> He has raised up a horn of salvation for us
> in the house of his servant David
> (as he said through his holy prophets of long ago),
> salvation from our enemies and from the hand of all
> who hate us to show mercy to our fathers and to
> remember his holy covenant,
> the oath he swore to our father Abraham:
> to rescue us from the hand of our enemies,
> and to enable us to serve him without fear
> in holiness and righteousness before him all our
> days. And you, my child, will be called a
> prophet of the Most High; for you will go on
> before the Lord to prepare a way for him,
> to give his people the knowledge of salvation
> through the forgiveness of their sins,
> because of the tender mercy of our God,
> by which the rising sun will come to us from heaven
> to shine on those living in darkness and in the shadow
> of death, to guide our feet into the path of peace' "
>   (Luke 1:57 79).

PART TWO

THE POWER OF PRAISE AND THANKSGIVING

8. THE POWER OF PRAISE AND THANKSGIVING

THE DEFEAT OF THE MOABITES AND AMMONITES

«After this, the Moabites and the Ammonites with some of the Meunites came to make war on Jehoshaphat.

Some men came and told Jehoshaphat, 'A vast army is coming against you from Edom, from the other side of the sea. It is already in Hazazon Tamar' (that is, Engedi). Alarmed, Jehoshaphat resolved to enquire of the Lord, and he proclaimed a fast for all Judah. The people of Judah came together to seek help from the Lord; indeed, they came from every town in Judah to seek him.

Then Jehoshaphat stood up in the assembly of Judah and Jerusalem at the temple of the Lord in front of the new courtyard and said:

> 'O Lord, God of our fathers, are you not the God
> who is in heaven? You rule over all the kingdoms
> of the nations. Power and might are in your hand,
> and no one can withstand you. O our God, did you
> not drive out the inhabitants of this land before your
> people Israel and give it for ever to the descendants
> of Abraham your friend? They have lived in it and
> have built in it a sanctuary for your name, saying, 'If
> calamity comes upon us, whether the sword of
> judgment, or plague or famine, we will stand in your

presence before this temple that bears your Name and will cry out to you in our distress, and you will hear us and save us.'

'But now here are men from Ammon, Moab and Mount Seir, whose territory you would not allow Israel to invade when they came from Egypt; so they turned away from them and did not destroy them. See how they are repaying us by coming to drive us out of the possession you gave us as an inheritance. O our God, will you not judge them? For we have no power to face this vast army that is attacking us. We do not know what to do, but our eyes are upon you.'

All the men of Judah, with their wives and children and little ones, stood there before the Lord.

The Spirit of the Lord came upon Jahaziel son of Zechariah, the son of Benaiah the son of Jeiel, the son of Mattaniah, a Levite and descendant of Asaph, as he stood in the assembly.

He said, 'Listen, King Jehoshaphat and all who live in Judah and Jerusalem! This is what the Lord says to you: 'Do not be afraid or discouraged because of this vast army. For the battle is not yours, but God's. Tomorrow march down against them. They will be climbing up by the Pass of Ziz, and you

will find them at the end of the gorge in the Desert
of Jeruel. You will not have to fight this battle. Take
up your positions; stand firm and see the deliverance
the Lord will give you, O Judah and Jerusalem. Do
not be afraid; do not be discouraged. Go out to face
them tomorrow, and the Lord will be with you.'

Jehoshaphat bowed with his face to the ground, and
all the people of Judah and Jerusalem fell down in
worship before the Lord. Then some Levites from
the Kohathites and Korahites stood up and praised
the Lord, the God of Israel, with a very loud voice.

Early in the morning they left for the Desert of
Tekoa. As they set out, Jehoshaphat stood and said,
'Listen to me, Judah and the people of Jerusalem!
Have faith in the Lord your God and you will be
upheld; have faith in his prophets and you will be
successful.' After consulting the people, Jehoshaphat
appointed men to sing to the Lord and to praise him
for the splendour of his holiness as they went out at
the head of the army, saying:

'Give thanks to the Lord,
for his love endures for ever.'

As they began to sing and praise, the Lord set
ambushes against the men of Ammon and Moab
 and Mount Seir who were invading Judah, and they

were defeated. The men of Ammon and Moab
rose up against the men from Mount Seir to destroy
and annihilate them. After they finished slaughtering
the men from Seir, they helped to destroy one
another.

When the men of Judah came to the place that
overlooks the desert and looked towards the vast
army, they saw only dead bodies lying on the ground;
no-one had escaped. So Jehoshaphat and his men
went to carry off their plunder, and they found
among them a great amount of equipment and
clothing and also articles of value more than they
could take away. There was so much plunder that
it took three days to collect it; On the fourth day
they assembled in the Valley of Beracah, where
they praised the Lord. This is why it is called the
Valley of Beracah to this day.

Then, led by Jehoshaphat, all the men of Judah and
Jerusalem returned joyfully to Jerusalem, for the
Lord had given them cause to rejoice over their
enemies. They entered Jerusalem and went to the
temple of the Lord with harps and lutes and trumpets.

The fear of God came upon all the kingdoms of the
countries when they heard how the Lord had fought
against the enemies of Israel"

(2 Chronicles 20:1 29).

PRAISE AND THANKSGIVING ARE POWERFUL WEAPONS

We state clearly that praise and thanksgiving to the Lord are mighty weapons. They can be used to accomplish great exploits in spiritual warfare. We bless the Lord that He has ordained it to be so.

We also want to say that praise and thanksgiving should not be thought of as some charm or magic formula that can be brought in by anyone under any circumstance, and magic results will be produced. The children of Israel thought that they could live out of harmony with the Lord and His will, and be fit for battle with the enemy, and that the ark of the Lord could be brought to the battlefront and it would produce or work wonders. They discovered that God is very consistent and that He would allow even the ark of the covenant to be captured by the enemies of Israel.

We must therefore understand that praise and thanksgiving work for people who are pure in heart, who call upon God out of a pure heart and obey Him in all things. It is then that praise can be used by the Lord to bring limitless blessing on the people of God.

THE ENEMY OF ISRAEL

Jehoshaphat and Judah had a formidable enemy a vast army made up of people from Ammon, Moab and Mount Seir.

The enemy was a multitude. The enemy was already on the move. He had advanced as far as Engedi.

JEHOSHAPHAT KNEW GOD AND KNEW HOW TO HANDLE CRISIS SITUATIONS

When Jehoshaphat heard about the massive enemy who was already approaching, he was alarmed. He did not pretend that all was all right. He did not just say, «Praise the Lord, all will be alright.» He was alarmed. Alarmed, he did not turn to himself or to his army or to his allies. He resolved to enquire of the Lord! He knew that God had the answer. He knew that only God had the answer.

He knew the power of fasting. He knew that fasting was a way of humbling oneself in order to seek the Lord. He therefore declared a fast for all Judah. He did not decide to fast alone. He knew that it was the battle of the entire tribe and that all should fast. He gathered the people together to seek help from the Lord. He got the people to come from every town in Judah to seek the Lord for help.

Jehoshaphat knew God, the history of the people of God, the promises of God, the power of God, and the size of the enemy. He prayed from this multifaced knowledge:

- O Lord, God of our fathers, are You not the God who is in heaven?
- You rule over all the kingdoms of the nations.

- Power and might are in Your hand.
- No one can withstand You.
- You drove out the inhabitants of this land before Your   people Israel.
- You gave it for ever to the descendants of Abraham Your friend.
- They have lived in it.
- They have built a sanctuary for Your name in it.
- They had established that if they cried to God in their distress, he would hear them.
- The enemy was defeated by the Lord in the past.
- The enemy was acting unjustly.
- The enemy should be judged by the Lord; for Israel had no power over such a vast enemy.
- Israel did not know what to do.
- Israel's eyes were upon the Lord !

GOD SPOKE BACK TO JEHOSHAPHAT AND JUDAH

We have a God who speaks. The Spirit of the Lord came upon Jahaziel and the Lord spoke through him to the king and the people of Judah. The Lord told them:

> not to be afraid,
> not to be discouraged because of the vast army.
> The battle was not theirs.
> The battle was the Lord's.
> They were to go against them the following day.

Details were given as to where they would be.
They would not have to fight in this battle.
They were to take their positions.
They were to stand firm.
They would see the deliverance that the Lord would give them.
He insisted that they should not be afraid.
He insisted that they should not be discouraged.
He insisted that they were to go out the following day and face them.
He assured them that God would be with them.

JEHOSHAPHAT AND THE PEOPLE KNEW HOW TO RESPOND TO GOD

The Lord spoke. He did not tell them what to do immediately. There was freedom to act according to what was in their hearts. Jehoshaphat bowed with his face to the ground. All the people of Judah and Jerusalem fell before the Lord and worshipped. Some Kohathites and Korahites stood up and praised the Lord, the God of Israel, with a very loud voice.

They praised the Lord with a very loud voice. They could have praised the Lord in their hearts, very silently, silently, a little loudly, loudly, very loudly. They chose to praise the Lord very loudly.

It may be that very loud praise does something to God and to the devil that quiet praise cannot do. It is very likely that the power of praise is proportional to the volume. It is most likely something like the following:

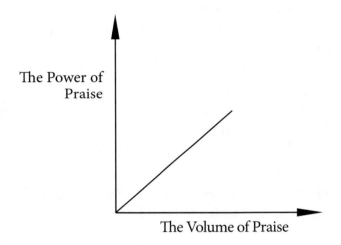

The Bible encourages loud praise. Below are some references of loud praise:

1.   Psalm 32:11 (RSV). «Be glad in the Lord, and rejoice, O righteous, and shout for joy, all you upright in heart.»

2.   Psalm 35:18 «I will give you thanks in the great assembly; among throngs of people I will praise you.»

3.   Psalm 40:3 «He put a new song in my mouth, a hymn of praise to our God. Many will see and fear and put their trust in the Lord.» Many cannot see the praise in the heart, or silent praise!

4. Psalm 47:1 «Clap your hands, all you nations; shout to God with cries of joy.»

5. Psalm 51:15 «O Lord, open my lips, and my mouth will declare your praise.»

6. Psalm 57:9 «I will praise you, O Lord, among the nations; I will sing of you among the peoples.»

7. Psalm 66:8 «Praise our God, O peoples, let the sound of his praise be heard.»

The sound of silent praise cannot be heard!

To praise the Lord aloud is a public confession. The devil will prefer silent praise. Loud praise is a public proclamation that we prefer our God to him. It humiliates him and exalts our Lord. It brings joy to the Lord. If someone you loved made a broadcast of his love for you, it would bring joy to you, would it not? Loud praise brings joy to our God. Loud praise is powerful praise.

If Jehoshaphat had been offering the priase to God just to ease his conscience, he would have stopped there and said, «I have fulfilled the command to praise the Lord.» However, he was not acting a part. He was praising the Lord, and all Judah with him.

The next day, they obeyed and left for the Desert of Tekoa. As they set out, Jehoshaphat consulted the people and appointed men to sing to the Lord and to praise Him for the splendour of His holiness.

These singers went out at the head of the army. Their song was: «Give thanks to the Lord, for his love endures for ever.» So the army was led by Praise and Thanksgiving.

PRAISE AND THANKSGIVING TRIGGERED OFF THE ACT OF VICTORY

As we have seen, they worshipped the Lord and praised Him before moving to the battlefront. They were praising Him for the victory He had promised. They were acting in faith. They believed Him and so sang His praises in glorious expectation.

Some would say, «Let us wait and behold the victory before we praise the Lord.» They do not believe the Lord. They are afraid to risk on Him. They are afraid of ridiculing themselves. Such cannot see the great glory of God. Others might say, «Let us wait for victory first. Praise is costly. What if we praise and nothing happens? How shall we be compensated for our energies and time?» Such selfish hearts hold God in contempt. They cannot really praise God and they cannot behold His glory. May none of us be like that!

When they began to sing and praise, the Lord set ambushes against the enemy. The Lord was waiting for this special praise and thanksgiving that came from the frontline of the army. When He saw it, He acted at once and the enemy was destroyed.

Praise and thanksgiving did it!
Praise and thanksgiving are doing it.
Praise and thanksgiving will do it.

God did not act until praise and thanksgiving were poured
upon Him. The Lord saw their seeking Him, but waited.
      He saw their fast, but waited.
      He saw their assembling, but waited.

When the Lord saw their praise and thanksgiving, He could
not wait any longer. It is as if the Lord were looking for this
one thing: Praise and Thanksgiving!. It is as if praise and
thanksgiving were the catalyst, the indispensable element
without which victory could not be won. When praise and
thanksgiving came forth, God acted.

The Lord Jesus told the rich young ruler, «One thing you
lack ...» Could it be that you have fasted,
          praised,
          maintained a pure heart before the Lord,
and yet, one particular answer to prayer has not come?
Could it be that the Lord is saying to you: «One thing is
lacking the sacrifice of praise and thanksgiving»? Will you
not add that missing element and see what our God will do?

Will you not do it now? Will you not continue to do it until
the answer comes? The Lord will not delay longer. Honour
Him by a sacrifice of praise, and His heart will be satisfied
and He will act. Hallelujah!!!

POST VICTORY PRAISE AND THANKSGIVING

The heart of man is exposed by what he does after God has blessed him. There are many who are prepared to

- fast,
- pray,
- seek the Lord,
- walk in purity,
- consecrate all,
- praise the Lord in anticipation,

and, in every other way possible, try to show their sincerity towards God while they are seeking God's intervention in a situation. When God has acted, they withdraw very neatly and totally from fasting,

- praying,
- seeking the Lord,
- walking in purity,
- consecration of self and all,
- praising the Lord for what He has done.

Such cannot know the greater deliverance of the Lord.

Jehoshaphat and Judah were not like that. They praised the Lord and thanked Him before the battle. They praised and thanked Him during the battle. They also praised and thanked Him after the victory was won. The Bible says,

«On the fourth day, they assembled in the Valley of Beracah, where they praised the Lord.» Their praise gave the valley a name; for «Valley of Beracah» means «Valley of Praise.»

That was not all. When they returned to Jerusalem, «They went to the temple of the Lord with harps and lutes and trumpets,» obviously to continue in praise and thanksgiving to the Lord! Glory be to the Lord!! That is what it was supposed to be. That is what it is supposed to be.

There was power in Praise and Thanksgiving.
There is power in Praise and Thanksgiving.
There will always be power in Praise and Thanksgiving.
Glory, glory, glory be to the Lord!

Amen.

09. THE POWER OF PRAISE AND THANKSGIVING 2

THE CONQUEST OF JERICHO

As the Children of Israel moved into the Promised Land, the first city that they had to conquer was Jericho. The future depended very much on what would happen in their conflict with Jericho. The Lord God said to Joshua, "See, I have delivered Jericho into your hands, along with its king and its fighting men. March around the city once with all the armed men. Do this for six days. Make seven priests carry trumpets of rams' horns in front of the ark. On the seventh day, march around the city seven times, with the priests blowing the trumpets. When you hear them sound a long blast of the trumpet, make all the people give a loud shout; then the wall of the city will collapse and the people will go up, every man straight in.'

So Joshua son of Nun called the priests and said to them, 'Take up the ark of the covenant of the Lord and make seven priests carry trumpets in front of it.' And he ordered the people, 'Advance! March around the city, with the armed guard going ahead of the ark of the Lord.'

When Joshua had spoken to the people, the seven priests carrying the seven trumpets before the Lord went forward, blowing their trumpets, and the ark of the Lord's covenant followed them. The armed guard marched ahead of the priests who blew the trumpets, and the rear guard followed the ark. All this time the trumpets were sounding. But Joshua had commanded the people, 'Do not give a war cry, do not raise your voices, do not say a word until the day I tell you to shout. Then shout!' So he had the ark of the Lord carried around the city, circling it once. The people returned to the camp and spent the night there.

Joshua got up early the next morning and the priests took up the ark of the Lord. The seven priests carrying the seven trumpets went forward, marching before the ark of the Lord and blowing the trumpets. The armed men went ahead of them and the rear guard followed the ark of the Lord, while the trumpets kept sounding. So on the second day they marched around the city once and returned to the camp. They did this for six days.

On the seventh day, they got up at daybreak and marched around the city seven times in the same manner, except that on that day they circled the city seven times. The seventh time around, when the priests sounded the trumpet blast, Joshua commanded the people, 'Shout! For the Lord has given you the city! The city and all that is in it are to be devoted to the Lord. Only Rahab the prostitute and all who are with her in her house shall be spared, because she hid the spies we sent. But keep away from the devoted things, so that you will not bring about your own destruction by taking any of them. Otherwise you will make the camp of Israel liable to destruction and bring trouble on it. All silver and gold and the articles of bronze and iron are sacred to the Lord and must go into his treasury.'

When the trumpet sounded, the people shouted, and at the sound of the trumpet, when the people gave a loud shout, the wall collapsed; so every man charged straight in, and they took the city. They devoted the city to the Lord and destroyed with the sword every living thing in it   men and women, young and old, cattle, sheep and donkeys.

Joshua said to the two men who had spied out the land, 'Go into the prostitute's house and bring her out and all who belong to her, in accordance with your oath to her.' So the young men who had done the spying went in and brought out Rahab, her father and mother and brothers and all who belonged to her. They brought out her entire family and put them in a place outside the camp of Israel.

Then they burned the whole city and everything in it, but they put the silver and gold and the articles of bronze and iron into the treasury of the Lord's house. But Joshua spared Rahab the prostitute, with her family and all who belonged to her, because she hid the men Joshua had sent as spies to Jericho and she lives among the Israelites to this day.

At that time Joshua pronounced this solemn oath: 'Cursed before the Lord is the man who undertakes to rebuild this city, Jericho: 'At the cost of his firstborn son will he lay the foundations; at the cost of his youngest will he set up its gates'" (Joshua 6:2 26).

Two elements were crucial for the conquest of Jericho. The first one was obedience. The second one was praise.

OBEDIENCE

There is a sense in which the battle against Jericho was a simple battle. There is another sense in which it was far from easy. There are few chapters in the Bible that are so pregnant with instructions that must be obeyed. Let us look at just a few of them:

1. March around the city once with all the armed men.
2. Do this for six days.
3. Make seven priests carry trumpets of rams' horns in front of the ark.
4. On the seventh day, march around the city seven times with the priests blowing the trumpets.
5. When you hear them sound a long blast on the trumpets, make all the people give a loud shout.
6. The wall of the city will collapse.
7. The people will go up, every man straight in.

These were the general instructions. Let us look at the detailed instructions:

1. Take up the ark of the covenant of the Lord.
2. Make seven priests carry trumpets in front of it.
3. Advance.
4. March around the city, with the armed guards going ahead of the ark.
5. Do not give a war cry.
6. Do not raise your voices.
7. Do not say a word until the day I tell you to shout.
8. Then shout.
9. Etc.

Spiritual warfare is God's warfare. Those who are involved must hear Him clearly and carry out His instructions to the letter. Disobedience is fatal. Achan disobeyed and perished.

Joshua ensured that the city was completely destroyed and, because it was devoted to the Lord, meaning that it was irrevocably given over to the Lord, he ensured that no one would ever rebuild it by cursing would be builders. In that way it would always belong to the Lord and never belong to any man.

There is an urgent need for a radical return to obeying the Lord in all things. There is no substitute for this.

PRAISE AND THANKSGIVING

The Bible says, «All this time the trumpets were sounding» (Joshua 6:9), and again, «While the trumpets kept sounding»(Joshua 6:13). It is as if to say, "Praise and Thanksgiving kept flowing to the Lord."

As the day of victory came all was ready. What caused the walls of Jericho to collapse? For sure, it was the power of the Lord. God's might, God's power did it. What was man's contribution? The Bible says, «WHEN THE TRUMPETS SOUNDED, THE PEOPLE SHOUTED, AND AT THE SOUND OF THE TRUMPET, WHEN THE PEOPLE GAVE A LOUD SHOUT, THE WALL COLLAPSED; SO EVERY MAN CHARGED STRAIGHT IN, AND THEY TOOK THE CITY» (Joshua 6:20).

> The marching was done.
> The ark of the covenant of the Lord was there.
> Joshua was there.
> The people were there.

However, without the sounding of the trumpets and the shouting of the people, the wall would not have collapsed, and Jericho would not have been taken.

Why was that so? It was so because the Lord had ordained that when the praise that came to Him from the trumpets' sound and the praise that came to Him from the shouts of the people reached Him, He would release His power that would cause the wall to collapse. When those praises reached Him, He acted at once and the wall collapsed.

The Lord is waiting for the praise and the thanksgiving of His children to flow to Him ceaselessly,
   - at all times,
   - in all circumstances,
   - in everything,
   - for everything,
and then He will release His power in the most limitless way and do the most unparalleled work of all time for His glory and His Church's edification.

The question is, «Will He receive such praise and thanksgiving?» The question is, «Will you rise and begin to do all you can to ensure that, as far as it depends on you, such praise and thanksgiving flow to Him? Praise the Lord!

10. THE POWER OF PRAISE AND THANKSGIVING 3

THE DEFEAT OF THE MIDIANITES BY GIDEON

The Lord had sent Gideon to conquer the Midianites. Gideon marshalled an army of thirty two thousand. But the Lord said to Gideon, "You have too many men for me to deliver Midian into their hands. In order that Israel may not boast against me that her own strength has saved her, announce now to the people, 'Anyone who trembles with fear may turn back and leave Mount Gilead.' So twenty two thousand men left, while ten thousand remained.

But the Lord said to Gideon, «There are still too many men. Take them down to the water, and I will sift them out for you there. If I say, 'This one shall go with you,' he shall go; but if I say, 'This one shall not go with you,' he shall not go."

So Gideon took the men down to the water. There the Lord told him, 'Separate those who lap the water with their tongues like a dog from those who kneel down to drink.' Three hundred men lapped with their hands to their mouths. All the rest got down their knees to drink.

The Lord said to Gideon, 'With the three hundred men that lapped I will save you and give the Midianites into your hands. Let all the other men go, each to his own place.' So Gideon sent the rest of the Israelites to their tents but kept the three hundred, who took over the provisions and trumpets of the others....

When Gideon heard the dream and its interpretation, he worshipped God. He returned to the camp of Israel and called out, 'Get up! The Lord has given the Midianite camp into your hands.' Dividing the three hundred men into three companies, he placed trumpets and empty jars in the hands of all of them, with torches inside.

'Watch me,' he told them. 'Follow my lead. When I get to the edge of the camp, do exactly as I do. When I and all who are with me blow our trumpets, then from all around the camp blow yours and shout, 'For the Lord and for Gideon.'

Gideon and the hundred men with him reached the edge of the camp at the beginning of the middle watch, just after they had changed the guard. They blew their trumpets and broke the jars that were in their hands. The three companies blew the trumpets and smashed the jars. Grasping the torches in their left hands and holding in their right hands the trumpets they were to blow, they shouted, 'A sword for the Lord and for Gideon!' While each man held his position around the camp, all the Midianites ran, crying out as they fled.

When the three hundred trumpets sounded, the Lord caused the men throughout the camp to turn to each other with their swords. The army fled to Beth Shittah towards Zererah as far as the border of Abel Meholah near Tabbath» (Judges 7:2 22).

The battle was won on the basis of discipline, courage and praise. Those who were fearful were eliminated from the battle. Those who were indulgent were also eliminated. It is striking that thousands of people were eliminated just because of an indulgent way of drinking water. A soldier could lap water like a dog with all his equipment and provision on his back. However, those who knelt down to drink had to put down their loads. They wanted comfort, ease and the like. They were indulgent and, consequently, eliminated. Indulgent people have no place in the army of God. The Apostle Paul said, «Every athlete exercises self control in all things» (1 Corinthians 9:25 RSV). He again said, «But I pommel my body and subdue it, lest after preaching to others I myself should be disqualified» (1 Corinthians 9:27 RSV).

So you need to wake up and throw away all the indulgent practices in your life that stand between you and God's best for your life. Will you begin right now?

PRAISE AND THANKSGIVING

The battle was won when they blew their trumpets and broke the jars that were in their hands. The decisive moment came with the blowing of the trumpets. The Bible says, «WHEN THE THREE HUNDRED TRUMPETS SOUNDED, THE LORD CAUSED THE MEN (MIDIANITES) THROUGHOUT THE CAMP TO TURN TO EACH OTHER WITH THEIR SWORDS» (Judges 7:22). Without the trumpets' sound all would have been lost.

So there were the shouts that went up to the Lord as praise. Then there was the noise of praise from jars being broken.

Finally, there were the trumpets' sound.
Then victory was won.

Glory be to God !

PRAISE AND THANKSGIVING AND MIRACLES

In the two preceding chapters and in this one, praise and thanksgiving brought down the supernatural power of God into battlefronts. It then seems that praise and thanksgiving and miracles are linked. When the Lord receives praise and thanksgiving from a pure heart, He releases His miracle working power into the situation. We can represent it as follows:

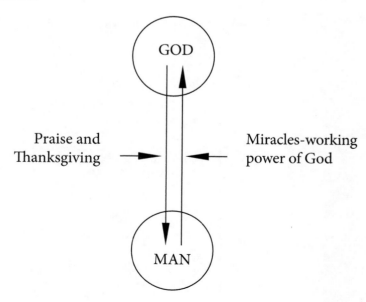

If that be the case, and I believe it is the case, then the following can be said:

May we then rise up and build strong and effective personal, group, national and international Ministries of Praise and Thanksgiving, and then we shall see God's miracle working power released in our lives, in our churches, in our nations and world wide to the glory of God the Father!

Praise the Lord! Amen.

PART THREE

DAVID AND THE MINISTRY OF PRAISE AND THANKSGIVING

11. GOD'S COMMAND THROUGH DAVID
TO PRAISE AND GIVE THANKS.

There are commands of the Lord that are given once or twice in the entire Bible, and the people of God feel totally obliged to obey these. This is the correct attitude; for the Lord does not need to speak a second time before He is obeyed. Those who love Him obey His every command. They also obey the slightest desire of His heart.

If a person feels compelled to obey the other commands of the Lord, then he should feel under even greater obligation to obey the command to praise and thank the Lord, because the command is given in very many Bible passages. The repetition of the command over and over shows us that the Lord attaches primary importance to its obedience. The Bible says:

1. 01. From the lips of children and infants you have ordained praise because of your enemies, to silence the foe and the avenger. (Psalm 8:2).

2. I will praise you, O Lord, with all my heart; I will tell of all your wonders. I will be glad and rejoice in you; I will sing praise to your name, O Most High. (Psalm 9:1 2).

3. Sing praises to the Lord, enthroned in Zion; proclaim among the nations what he has done. (Psalm 9:11)

4. Ascribe to the Lord, O mighty ones, ascribe to the Lord glory and strength. Ascribe to the Lord the glory due to his name; worship the Lord in the splendour of his holiness. (Psalm 29:1 2).

5. Sing to the Lord, you saints of his; praise his holy name. For his anger lasts only a moment, but his favour lasts a lifetime; weeping may remain for a night, but rejoicing comes in the morning.(Psalm 30:4 5).

6. Sing joyfully to the Lord, you righteous; it is fitting for the upright to praise him. Praise the Lord with the harp; make music to him on the ten stringed lyre. Sing to him a new song; play skilfully, and shout for joy. (Psalm 33:1 3).

7. Clap your hands, all you nations; shout to God with cries of joy. (Psalm 47:1).

8. Great is the Lord, and most worthy of praise, is the city of our God, his holy mountain. (Psalm 48:1).

9. Shout with joy to God, all the earth! Sing the glory of his name; make his praise glorious! Say to God, «How awesome are your deeds! So great is your power that your enemies cringe before you. All the earth bows down to you; they sing praises to you, they sing praises to your name. (Psalm 66:1 4).

10. Praise our God, O peoples, let the sound of his praise be heard; he has preserved our lives and kept our feet from slipping. (Psalm 66:8 9).

11. May the peoples praise you, O God; may all the peoples praise you. May the nations be glad and sing for joy, for you rule the people justly and guide the nations of the earth. May the peoples praise you, O God; may all the peoples praise you. Then the land will yield its harvest, and God, our God, will bless us. God will bless us, and all the ends of the earth will fear him. (Psalm 67:3 7).

12. Sing to God, sing praise to his name, extol him who rides on the clouds   his name is the Lord   and rejoice before him. (Psalm 68:4).

13. Praise be to the Lord God, the God of Israel, who alone does marvellous deeds. Praise be to his glorious name for ever; may the whole earth be filled with his glory. Amen and Amen. (Psalm 72:18 19).

14. Sing for joy to God our strength; shout aloud to the God of Jacob! Begin the music, strike the tambourine, play the melodious harp and lyre. Sound the horn at the New Moon, and when the moon is full, on the day of our feast; this is a secret for Israel, and an ordinance of the God of Jacob. (Psalm 81:1 4).

15. Sing to the Lord a new song; sing to the Lord, all the earth. Sing to the Lord, praise his name; proclaim his salvation day after day. Declare his glory among the nations, his marvellous deeds among all peoples. For great is the Lord and most worthy of praise; he is to be feared above all gods. For all the gods of the nations are idols, but the Lord made the heavens. Splendour

and majesty are before him; strength and glory are in his sanctuary. Ascribe to the Lord, O families of the nations, ascribe to him glory and strength. Ascribe to the Lord the glory due to his name; bring an offering and come into his courts. Worship the Lord in the splendour of his holiness; tremble before him, all the earth. Say among the nations, «The Lord reigns.» The world is firmly established, it cannot be moved; he will judge the peoples with equity. Let the heavens rejoice, let the earth be glad; let the sea resound, and all that is in it; let the fields be jubilant, and everything in them. Then all the trees of the forest will sing for joy; they will sing before the Lord, for he comes, he comes to judge the earth. He will judge the world in righteousness and the peoples in his truth. (Psalm 96:1 13).

16. Sing to the Lord a new song, for he has done marvellous things; his right hand and his holy arm have worked salvation for him. (Psalm 98:1).

17. Give thanks to the Lord, call on His name; make known among the nations what he has done. Sing to him, sing praises to him; tell of all his wonderful acts. Glory in his holy name; let the hearts of those who seek the Lord rejoice. (Psalm 105:1 3).

18. Praise the Lord. Give thanks to the Lord, for he is good; his love endures for ever. (Psalm 106:1).

19. Give thanks to the Lord, for he is good; his love endures for ever. (Psalm 107:1).

20. Praise the Lord. Praise, O servants of the Lord, praise the name of the Lord. Let the name of the Lord be praised, both now and for evermore. From the rising of the sun to the place where it sets, the name of the Lord is to be praised. (Psalm 113:1 3).

21. Praise the Lord, all you nations; extol him, all you peoples. For great is his love towards us, and the faithfulness of the Lord endures for ever. Praise the Lord. (Psalm 117:1 2).

22. Give thanks to the Lord, for he is good; his love endures for ever. Let Israel say: «His love endures for ever.» Let the house of Aaron say: «His love endures for ever.» Let those who fear the Lord say: «His love endures for ever» (Psalm 118:1 4).

23. Praise the Lord, all you servants of the Lord who minister by night in the house of the Lord. Lift up your hands in the sanctuary and praise the Lord. (Psalm 134:1 2).

24. Praise the Lord. Praise the name of the Lord; Praise him, you servants of the Lord, you who minister in the house of the Lord, in the courts of the house of our God. Praise the Lord, for he is good; sing praise to his name, for that is pleasant. For the Lord has chosen Jacob to be his own, Israel to be his treasured possession. (Psalm 135:1 4).

25. Give thanks to the Lord, for he is good. His love endures for ever... to him who alone does great wonders,

His love endures for ever... to him who led his people through the desert... to the One who remembered us in our low estate... and freed us from our enemies... and who gives food to every creature... Give thanks to the God of heaven. His love endures for ever. (Psalm 136:1 26).

26. Praise the Lord. Praise the Lord from the heavens, praise him in the heights above. Praise him all his angels, praise him, all his heavenly hosts. Praise him, sun and moon, praise him, all you shining stars. Praise him, you highest heavens and you waters above the skies. Let them praise the name of the Lord, for he commanded and they were created. He set them in place for ever and ever; he gave a decree that will never pass away. Praise the Lord from the earth, you great sea creatures and all ocean depths, lightning and hail, snow and clouds, stormy winds that do his bidding, you mountains and all hills, fruit trees and all cedars, wild animals and all cattle, small creatures and flying birds; kings of the earth and all nations, you princes and all rulers on earth, young men and maidens, old men and children. Let them praise the name of the Lord, for his name alone is exalted; his splendour is above the earth and the heavens. He has raised up for his people a horn, the praise of all his saints, of Israel, the people close to his heart. Praise the Lord. (Psalm 148:1 14).

27. Praise the Lord. Sing to the Lord a new song, his praise in the assembly of the saints. Let Israel rejoice

in their Maker; let the people of Zion be glad in their King. Let them praise his name with dancing and make music to him with tambourine and harp. For the Lord takes delight in his people; he crowns the humble with salvation. Let the saints rejoice in this honour and sing for joy on their beds. May the praise of the Lord be in their mouths and a double edged sword in their hands, to inflict vengeance on the nations and punishment on the people, to bind their kings with fetters, their nobles with shackles of iron, to carry out the sentence written against them. This is the glory of all his saints. Praise the Lord. (Psalm 149:1 9).

28. Praise the Lord. Praise God in his sanctuary; praise him in his mighty heavens. Praise him for his acts of power; praise him for his surpassing greatness. Praise him with the sounding of the trumpet, praise him with the harp and the lyre, praise him with tambourine and dancing, praise him with the strings and flute, praise him with the clash of cymbals, praise him with resounding cymbals. Let everything that has breath praise the Lord. Praise the Lord. (Psalm 150:1 6).

WHO IS COMMANDED TO PRAISE AND THANK THE LORD?

The following are commanded to praise and thank the Lord:

01. mighty ones
02. saints.
03. righteous ones.
04. the upright.
04. all nations.
05. all the earth.
06. peoples.
07. all the peoples.
08. the whole earth.
09. Israel.
10. the sea.
11. all that is in the sea.
12. all the trees of the forest.
13. those who seek the Lord.
14. servants of the Lord.
15. all his angels.
16. all his heavenly hosts.
17. the sun.
18. the moon.
19. the stars.
20. the highest heavens.
21. the waters above the skies.
22. the sea creatures.
23. all ocean depths.

24. the lightning.
25. hail.
26. snow.
27. clouds.
28. stormy winds.
29. mountains.
30. all hills.
31. fruit trees.
32. all cedars.
33. wild animals.
34. all cattle.
35. small creatures.
36. flying birds.
37. kings of the earth.
38. princes.
39. rulers on earth.
40. young men.
41. maidens.
42. old men.
43. children.
44. everything that has breath.

You can immediately see that the command to praise the Lord involves you. You cannot escape. Inanimate objects are already praising the Lord. Animals are already praising the Lord. The whole creation is praising and thanking the Lord. Can you afford to be the exception? Certainly not. Begin today to thank Him and praise His glorious name.

WHAT REASONS ARE GIVEN FOR PRAISING AND THANKING THE LORD?

The following are some of the reasons advanced for praising and thanking the Lord:

1. Because He silenced the foe and the avenger.
2. Because of all His wonders.
3. Because of what He has done.
4. Because of the splendour of his holiness.
5. For His anger lasts only a moment.
6. For his favour lasts a lifetime.
7. For His preservation of life.
8. For keeping feet from slipping.
9. For His just ruling of the people.
10. For His guidance of the nations of the earth.
11. For He alone does marvellous deeds.
12. For His greatness.
13. For making the heavens.
14. For His reign.
15. Because He has done marvellous things.
16. Because He is good.
17. Because His love endures for ever.
18. Because His love towards us is great.
19. Because of His surpassing greatness.

HOW IS HE TO BE PRAISED AND THANKED ?

The Lord is to be praised and thanked by:

1. Singing.
2. Clapping the hands.
3. Shouting with joy.
4. Extolling His great name.
5. Striking the tambourine.
6. Playing the melodious harp.
7. Playing the melodious lyre.
8. Sounding the ram's horn.
9. Worshipping the Lord.
10. Falling before Him.
11. Standing before Him.
12. Lifting up hands in His presence.
13. Dancing.
14. Sounding the trumpet.
15. Clashing cymbals.
16. Resounding cymbals.
17. Playing strings.
18. Sounding the flute.

12. DAVID'S COMMITMENT TO A LIFE OF PRAISE AND THANKSGIVING

David was committed to praise and thanksgiving. He said:

«O Lord, our Lord,
how majestic is your name in all the earth!
You have set your glory
above the heavens.
From the lips of children and infants
you have ordained praise
because of your enemies,
to silence the foe and the avenger.
When I consider your heavens,
the work of your fingers,
the moon and the stars,
which you have set in place,
what is man that you are mindful of him,
the son of man that you care for him?
You made him a little lower than the heavenly beings
and crowned him with glory and honour.
You made him ruler over the works of your hands;
you put everything under his feet:
all flocks and herds,
and the beasts of the field,
the birds of the air, and the fish of the sea,
all that swim the paths of the seas.
O Lord, our Lord,
how majestic is your name in all the earth!"
    (Psalm 8:1 9).

He continued to say:

> I will praise you, O Lord, with all my heart;
> I will tell of your wonders.
> I will be glad and rejoice in you;
> I will sing praise to your name, O Most High.
> (Psalm 9:1 2).

And,

> I will exalt you, O Lord,
> for you lifted me out of the depth
> and did not let my enemies gloat over me.
> (Psalm 30:1).

And,

> I will extol the Lord at all times;
> his praise will always be on my lips.
> (Psalm 34:1).

He continued:

> «Praise awaits you, O God, in Zion;
> to you our vows will be fulfilled»
> (Psalm 65:1).

And,

> «I will praise God's name in song
> and glorify him with thanksgiving.
> This will please the Lord more than an ox,
> more than a bull with its horns and hoofs»
> (Psalm 69:30 31).

And,

> But as for me, I shall always have hope;
> I will praise you more and more.
> My mouth will tell of your righteousness,
> of your salvation all day long,
> though I know not its measure.
> I will come and proclaim your mighty acts,
> O Sovereign Lord;
> I will proclaim your righteousness, yours alone.
> Since my youth, O God, you have taught me,
> and to this day I declare your marvellous deeds.
> (Psalm 71:14 17).

And,

> «I will praise you with the harp
> for your faithfulness, O my God;
> I will sing praise to you with the lyre,
> O Holy One of Israel.
> My lips will shout for joy
> when I sing praise to you
> I, whom you have redeemed.
> My tongue will tell of your righteous acts all day
> long, for those who wanted to harm
> me have been put to shame and confusion»
> (Psalm 71:22 24).

And,

> «I will sing of the Lord's great love for ever;
> with my mouth I will make your faithfulness known
> through all generations.

I will declare that your love stands firm for ever,
that you established your faithfulness in heaven
itself» (Psalm 89:1 2).

And,

"I will say of the Lord, 'He is my refuge and my
fortress, my God, in whom I trust' "
(Psalm 91:2).

And,

«I will sing of your love and justice;
to you, O Lord, I will sing praise»
(Psalm 101:1).

And,

«Praise the Lord.
I will extol the Lord with all my heart
in the council of the upright and in the assembly»
(Psalm 111:1).

And,

«I will praise you, O Lord, with all my heart;
before the "gods" I will sing your praise.
I will bow down towards your holy temple
and will praise your name
for your love and your faithfulness,
for you have exalted above all things
your name and your word"
(Psalm 138:1 2).

And,

«I will exalt you, my God the King;
I will praise your name for ever and ever.

> Every day I will praise you
> and extol your name for ever and ever"
> (Psalm 145:1 2).

And,

> «Praise the Lord.
> Praise the Lord, O my soul;
> I will praise the Lord all my life;
> I will sing praise to my God as long as I live"
> (Psalm 146:1 2).

David committed himself to praise the Lord
>   with all his heart,
>   at all times,
>   in song,
>   with thanksgiving,
>   more and more,
>   with harp,
>   with lyre,
>   all day long,
>   for ever.

He did not only commit himself to it. He acted out his commitment. May we follow his example and then we shall be as blessed as he was; as he is!

13. DAVID'S PRACTICE OF PRAISE AND THANKSGIVING

There are people who make commitments but do not live out their commitments. We have seen that David committed himself to a life of praise and thanksgiving. In this chapter we shall see that he actually lived out his commitment.

When the Lord delivered him from all his enemies and from the hand of Saul, he praised and thanked the Lord, saying:

> «The Lord is my rock, my fortress and my deliverer;
> my God is my rock, in whom I take refuge,
> my shield and the horn of my salvation.
> He is my stronghold, my refuge and my saviour
> from violent men you saved me.
> I call to the Lord, who is worthy of praise;
> and I am saved from my enemies..."
> (2 Samuel 22:2 51).

He again praised and thanked the Lord as follows:

> "The Lord lives! Praise be to my Rock!
> Exalted be God my Saviour!
> He is the God who avenges me,
> who subdues nations under me,
> who saves me from my enemies.
> You exalted me above my foes;
>
> from violent men you rescued me.
> Therefore I will praise you among the nations,

O Lord;
I will sing praises to your name"
(Psalm 18:46 49).

He confessed,

«Seven times a day I praise you for your
righteous laws» (Psalm 119:164).

He proclaimed,

«Praise the Lord, O my soul.
O Lord my God, you are very great;
you are clothed with splendour and majesty»
(Psalm 104:1).

He proclaimed,

«The Lord reigns,
let the nations tremble;
he sits enthroned between the cherubim,
let the earth shake.
Great is the Lord in Zion,
he is exalted over all the nations»
(Psalm 99:1 2).

Again he confessed,

«The Lord reigns, he is robed in majesty;
the Lord is robed in majesty
and is armed with strength.

The world is firmly established;
it cannot be moved.
Your throne was established long ago;
you are from all eternity.
The seas have lifted up, O Lord,
the seas have lifted up their voice;
the seas have lifted up their pounding waves.
Mightier than the thunder of the great waters,
mightier than the breakers of the sea
the Lord on high is mighty.
Your statutes stand firm;
holiness adorns your house
for endless days, O Lord»
(Psalm 93:1 5).

He praised and thanked thus,

«Praise awaits you, O God, in Zion;
to you our vows will be fulfilled.
O you who hear prayer,
to you all men will come.
When we were overwhelmed with sins,
you forgave our transgressions.
Blessed are those you choose
and bring near to live in your courts!
We are filled with the good things of your house,
of your holy temple.
You answer us with awesome deeds of righteousness,
O God our Saviour,

the hope of all the ends of the earth
and of the farthest seas,
who formed the mountains by your power,
having armed yourself with strength,
who stilled the roaring of the seas,
the roaring of the waves,
and the turmoil of the nations,
Those living far away fear your wonders;
when morning dawns and evening fades
you call forth songs of joy» (Psalm 65:1 8).

David continued to praise and thank the Lord, saying:

«O God, you are my God, earnestly I seek you;
my soul thirsts for you, my body longs for you,
in a dry and weary land where there is no water.
I have seen you in the sanctuary
and beheld your power and your glory.
Because your love is better than life,
my lips will glorify you.
I will praise you as long as I live,
and in your name I will lift up my hands.
My soul will be satisfied as with the richest of foods;
with singing lips my mouth will praise you.
On my bed I remember you;
I think of you through the watches of the night.
Because you are my help,
I sing in the shadow of your wings"
(Psalm 63:1 7).

When the Lord told David that He, the Lord, would establish a house for him, David responded in praise and thanksgiving in the following words:

«Who am I, O Sovereign Lord, and what is my family, that you have brought me this far? And as if this were not enough in your sight, O Sovereign Lord, you have also spoken about the future of the house of your servant. Is this your usual way of dealing with man, O Sovereign Lord?

«What more can David say to you? For you know your servant, O Sovereign Lord. For the sake of your word and according to your will, you have done this great thing and made it known to your servant.

«How great you are, O Sovereign Lord! There is no one like you, and there is no God but you, as we have heard with our own ears» (2 Samuel 7:18 22).

So David practised what he taught. He lived his message. Glory be to the Lord! May we too, like him, live all that we invite people to do!   Amen.

14. DAVID'S APPOINTMENT OF PEOPLE TO OFFER PRAISE AND THANKSGIVING TO THE LORD GOD

David was not content to sing praises and thanksgiving to the Lord. He ensured that people were appointed to this task. The Bible says, «David told the leaders of the Levites to appoint their brothers as singers to sing joyful songs, accompanied by musical instruments: lyres, harps and cymbals. So the Levites appointed Heman son of Joel; from his brothers, Asaph son of Berekiah; and from their brothers the Merarites, Ethan son of Kushaiah; and with them their brothers next in rank: Zechariah, Jaaziel, Shemiramoth, Jehiel, Unni, Eliab, Benaiah, Maaseiah, Mattithiah, Eliphelehu, Mikneiah, Obed Edom and Jeiel, the gatekeepers.

The musicians Heman, Asaph and Ethan were to sound the bronze cymbals; Zechariah, Aziel, Shemiramoth, Jehiel, Unni, Maaseiah and Benaiah were to play the lyres according to alamoth, and Mattithiah, Eliphelehu, Mikneiah, Obed Edom, Jeiel and Azaziah were to play the harps, directing according to sheminith. Kenaniah the head Levite was in charge of the singing; that was his responsibility because he was skilful at it»(1 Chronicles 15:16 22).

This was done in preparation for bringing back the ark of God to the tent he had pitched for it.

When the ark had been placed in the tent and the necessary sacrifices made, the Bible says, «He appointed some of the Levites to minister before the ark of the Lord, to make petitions, to give thanks, and to praise the Lord, the God of Israel: Asaph was the chief, Zechariah second, then Jeiel,... They were to sound the cymbals, and Benaiah and Jahaziel the priest were to blow trumpets regularly before the ark of the covenant of God.

That day David first committed to Asaph and his associates this psalm of thanks to the Lord:

> Give thanks to the Lord, call on his name;
> make known among the nations what he has done.
> Sing to him, sing praise to him;
> tell of his wonderful acts...”
> (1 Chronicles 16:4 36).

The Bible continues to say, «When David was old and full of years, he made his son Solomon king over Israel. He also gathered together all the leaders of Israel, as well as the priest and Levites. The Levites thirty years old or more were counted, and the total number of men was thirty eight thousand. David said, «Of these, twenty four thousand are to supervise the work of the temple of the Lord and six thousand are to be officials and judges. Four thousand are to be gatekeepers and four thousand are to praise the Lord with the musical instruments I have provided for that purpose» (1 Chronicles 23:1 5).

The Word of God continues to proclaim, «David, together with the commanders of the army, set apart some of the sons of Asaph, Heman and Jeduthun for the ministry of prophesying, accompanied by the harps, lyres and cymbals. Here is the list of the men who performed this service: From the sons of Asaph: Zaccur, Joseph, Nethaniah and Asarelah. The sons of Asaph were under the supervision of Asaph, who prophesied under the king's supervision. As for Jeduthun, from his sons: Gedaliah, Zeri, Jeshaiah, Shimei, Hashabiah and Mattithiah, six in all, under the supervision of their father Jeduthun, who prophesied, using the harp in thanksgiving and praising the Lord. As for Heman, from his sons: Bukkiah, Mattaniah, Uzziel, Shubael and Jerimoth; Hananiah, Hanani, Eliathah, Giddalti and Romamti Ezer; Joshbekashah, Mallothi, Hothir and Mahazioth. All these were sons of Heman the kings's seer. They were given to him through the promises of God to exalt him. God gave Heman fourteen sons and three daughters.

All these men were under the supervision of their fathers for the music of the temple of the Lord, with cymbals, lyres and harps, for the ministry at the house of God. Asaph, Jeduthun and Heman were under the supervision of the king. Along with their relatives   all of them trained and skilled in music for the Lord   they numbered two hundred and eighty eight. Young and old alike, teacher as well as student, cast lots for their duties» (1 Chronicles 25:1 8).

SOME THOUGHTS FOR OUR DAY

1. David's appointment of people to minister thanksgiving
    and praise to the Lord with musical instruments was an
    overflow of his own life that was given extensively to
    the Ministry of Praise and Thanksgiving with musical
    instruments. It was life because it flowed from life; it
    flowed from experience. Ministry should extend as an
    overflow of personal experience, and not as an imitation
    of what others are doing.

2. The quality of singing and playing of instruments was
    high. Time was put into it. Those gifted were identified
    and trained. Raw skill was not enough. Training of the
    untalented was not done. In the ministry, those who are
    gifted are to be trained to exercise their gifts. The Lord
    gives talents and gifts and expects those who have these
    to subject themselves to training in order to function at
    their best for the Lord.

3. There was order. The Bible says, «The sons of Asaph were
    under the supervision of Asaph, who prophesied under
    the king's supervision» (1 Chronicles 25:2). Does the
    notion of prophesying under supervision sound strange?
    Would it not limit or quench the Spirit ? Let us see what
    the New Testament says. It says, «If anyone speaks in
    a tongue, two or at the most three should speak, one
    at a time, and someone should interpret. If there is no
    interpreter, the speaker should keep quiet in the church
    and speak to himself and God. Two or three prophets

should speak and the others should weigh carefully what is said. And if a revelation comes to someone who is sitting down, the first speaker should stop. For you can all prophesy in turn so that everyone may be instructed and encouraged. The spirits of prophets are subject to the control of prophets. For God is not a God of disorder but of peace» (1 Corinthians 14:27 33).

a. It would seem that people are either spiritual and   disorganized or they are organized and unspiritual. God expects His people to be spiritual and orderly, to be   spiritual and organized.

4. There is a place for the Ministry of Praise and Thanksgiving with song and instruments. However, those to exercise that ministry must be: filled with the Holy Spirit, totally consecrated to the Lord, and delivered from the desire to sing for applause and the desire to make money. They are to minister to the Lord and they are to minister for the Lord. Radical holiness and radical purity must characterize such lives as well as the lives of those in the ministry of fasting, prayer, evangelism, pastoring and teaching. Yes, radical holiness and radical purity must characterize all who would serve the Lord of Holiness in any capacity. Without such holiness, purity and deliverance from the love of the world and the love of the things that are in the world, praise and thanksgiving become noise that is offensive to God.

5. Full time Ministers of Praise and Thanksgiving should have a place in the Church of the first born. It could be

that the Lord might call some members of the church to
give themselves to a life time Ministry of Praising and
Thanking the Lord for His mighty deeds in the Church.
Such should have inspiration from Anna who gave
herself exclusively to the ministry of fasting and praying.
(Luke 2:36 38).

Praise the Lord!

PART FOUR

COSTLY PRAISE
AND
THANKSGIVING

15. PRAISE AND THANKSGIVING:THE BEST
SACRIFICE TO THE LORD GOD   1

The Bible says:

> Rejoice always,
> Pray constantly,
> Give thanks in all circumstances,
> for this is the will of God in Christ Jesus for you.
> Do not quench the Spirit.
> (1 Thessalonians 5:16 19, RSV).

Be very careful, then, how you live   not as unwise but as
wise, making the most of every opportunity, because the
days are evil. Therefore do not be foolish, but understand
what the Lord's will is. Do not get drunk on wine, which
leads to debauchery. Instead, be filled with the Spirit. Speak
to one another with psalms, hymns and spiritual songs. Sing
and make music in your heart to the Lord, always giving
thanks to God the Father for everything, in the name of our
Lord Jesus Christ.   (Ephesians 5:15 20).

«The high priest carries the blood of animals into the Most
Holy Place as a sin offering, but the bodies are burned outside
the camp. And so Jesus also suffered outside the city gate to
make the people holy through his own blood. Let us, then,
go to him outside the camp, bearing the disgrace he bore.
For here we do not have an enduring city, but we are looking

for the city that is to come. Through Jesus, therefore, let us continually offer to God a sacrifice of praise the fruit of lips that confess his name. And do not forget to do good and to share with others, for with such sacrifices God is pleased»(Hebrews 13:11 16).

THREE COMMANDS TO BE OBEYED

In the verses which we have just read, there are a number of commands of our God to us. They are commands that He has given us to obey.

The first of these commands is: Rejoice always.
The second of these commands is: Pray constantly, pray without ceasing.
The third command is: Give thanks in all circumstances for everything.

So, rejoice always, pray without ceasing, and give thanks in all circumstances! These three together constitute a part of God's will for each believer. Yes, it is the will of God in Christ Jesus for you.

May we ask, «What is the will of God in Christ Jesus for you? We answer that the will of God in Christ Jesus for you is that you should:
rejoice always,
        pray without ceasing,
        give thanks in all circumstances for everything.

Then the Bible commands: «Do not quench the Spirit.» This means that if I do not rejoice, I quench the Spirit. If I do not pray without ceasing, I quench the Spirit. And if I do not give thanks in all circumstances and for everything, I quench the Spirit.

Because this book is on «The Ministry Of Praise And Thanksgiving», we are going to leave the first two commands aside and concentrate on the command to Give Thanks In Every Circumstance For Everything.

The Lord demands that we praise and thank Him

> when big good things happen to us,
> when small good things happen to us,
> for the routine things of our lives,
> when big bad things happen to us,
> when small bad things happen to us,
> in anticipation of small good things,
> and in anticipation of routine things happening to us.

This means that we shall praise and thank Him with exceedingly great joy for the events that cause exceedingly great joy to flow from us to the Lord. This is spontaneous praise that is not costly; for we beg God to receive it. In such circumstances, we are praising God for our own sake; for if we did not, we would feel like breaking.

This also means that we shall praise and thank Him with joy for the small good things that happen to us. We shall also thank Him with joy for the routines of our lives.

There will be major things to us which, at surface value, are great tragedies. We are to thank and praise the Lord for these as well. We are also to praise and thank the Lord for the small events that happen to us, whose surface evaluation indicates that they are for our hurt or they are actually hurting. It is here that an aspect of the sacrifice of praise and thanksgiving comes in we thank and praise the Lord for that which hurts, for that which causes pain. We thank and praise God when our natural being demands that we should not praise Him but should blame Him;

• some one else,
• ourselves, or
• circumstances.

God demands that instead of blaming Him, someone else, ourselves or circumstances, (and blaming any of these is sin) we should commit the righteousness of praising and thanking Him.

Such praise is a sacrifice because it is costly. You may ask, «What does it cost? What is sacrificed? The answer is simple: It costs self! Self is sacrificed!! When things happen which we do not like, the natural tendency is to blame,

       o complain,
       o criticize,
       o grumble,
       o murmur.

The self wants these very much; for they are the food on which self feeds! To praise the Lord instead of feeding self means that self is starved; self is sacrificed; self is denied attention; the attention that self wants is given to the Lord.

So the sacrifice of praise is the sacrifice of giving attention to the Lord instead of to self. This is costly. This can be very costly.

ALL PRAISE AND THANKSGIVING ARE A SACRIFICE

We have just said that praise and thanksgiving to the Lord when things that we do not want happen are a sacrifice because self is starved, ignored and put out of focus.

We want to say that all praise and thanksgiving are a sacrifice because, even when good things happen, the natural disposition is not to turn to the Lord in praise and thanksgiving, but to turn to self in praise and thanksgiving. The natural disposition is to say, «This good thing has happened to me, or I did this and that and behold, this is the result!"

Since praise and thanksgiving make God the Hero and not «self,» praise and thanksgiving, all praise and thanksgiving to the Lord are always a sacrifice. It is always the sacrifice of self. It is always costly. It never comes naturally except from hearts that know God deeply.

It has to be admitted that there are times when praise and thanksgiving to God for a good thing that has happened may even be offensive, because self wants credit for what has happened and the giving of that credit to someone else - to God - causes real offense. Thus all praise is a sacrifice. Praise and thanksgiving that are deep,
- wide,
- broad,
- enriching and

take time. It takes time to enter into God's presence and it takes time to stay there until detailed and thorough praise and thanksgiving have been offered to Him. This means that only those who are prepared to sacrifice sleeping time,
- eating time,
- relaxation time,
- planning time,
- working time, and
- asking time,

can carry out the Ministry of Praise and Thanksgiving. We insist that even among the saints who know something of spending time with God in prayer, very few are prepared to sacrifice long periods of asking time for praise and thanksgiving. It is difficult for too many believers to find quality time for prayer. Of the few who do find it, an even smaller percentage can sacrifice that time or a good portion of it for the Ministry of Praise and Thanksgiving. Those who are prepared to put aside time for praise and thanksgiving are making a sacrifice. They are making a costly sacrifice. They are making a sacrifice unto the Lord.

In prayer which consists of asking and receiving from God, we can ask, «Where is God's portion?» We can ask, «What does God get out of it for Himself? Is it not the exploitation of God by His own ?"

Is it not in praise and thanksgiving that God has His own share? May we not say that praise and thanksgiving are a ministry unto God? Is it then surprising that praise and thanksgiving should be valued so highly by God? Is it surprising that the Ministry of Praise and Thanksgiving are the highest level of service to the Lord? Is it also surprising that the enemy of our God has worked so hard to ensure that the saints are least developed in praise and thanksgiving, that the least time is given to praise and thanksgiving and that this great sin is hardly ever repented of and restitution carried out? Is it surprising that the enemy has worked so hard and thus gained grounds to hinder praise and thanksgiving, such that a praying person can invest one hundred hours into asking and is not prepared to give even a tithe of it, that is ten hours, to God in praise and thanksgiving?

Surely, the enemy has done harm, great harm. That harm needs to be undone. The tide must change. Praise and thanksgiving must become the central issue in prayer. The aspect of prayer that meets the needs of God must be given the first priority, and then all else will follow to the glory of God and the blessing of His children.

Praise the Lord!

«Offer to God a sacrifice of thanksgiving» (Psalm 50:14 RSV).

«He who brings thanksgiving as his sacrifice honours me» (Psalm 50:23 RSV).

«I will offer to thee the sacrifice of thanksgiving» (Psalm 116:17).

16. PRAISE AND THANKSGIVING: THE BEST SACRIFICE TO THE LORD GOD 2

The Bible commands, «Give thanks in all circumstances, for this is God's will for you in Christ Jesus»(1 Thessalonians 5:18). The Bible again says, «Always giving thanks to God the Father in everything, in the name of our Lord Jesus Christ» (Ephesians 5:20).

All circumstances are for praise and thanksgiving. This is God's will in Christ Jesus!

All time is for thanksgiving. This is God's will in Christ Jesus!!

Everything is the object for thanksgiving. This is God's will in Christ Jesus!!!

> Then the Bible adds, «Do not quench the Spirit» (1 Thessalonians 5:19 RSV).

From these passages we can say:

- Any time that I do not give thanks I quench the Spirit.
- Any circumstance in which I do not give thanks is a circumstance in which I quench the Spirit.
- Anything in which I do not give thanks to the Lord in the name of the Lord Jesus is a thing in which I quench the Spirit.

There is the constant choice between quenching the Spirit or giving thanks to the Father in the name of the Lord Jesus. That choice confronts every believer day in and day out, and the choice made determines whether the believer is going to continue to be filled with the Holy Spirit or he is going to continue without being filled with the Holy Spirit. Those who choose to give thanks to the Lord in every situation continue to be filled with the Holy Spirit. Those who choose not to give thanks quench the Spirit and become the losers!

In a difficult or nasty situation, the believer can choose to praise the Lord in the situation or he can choose to
 - complain,
 - murmur, or
 - grumble.

Complaining believers are spiritual fire extinguishers. They put out the Spirit's fire. Murmuring believers are spiritual fire extinguishers. They put out the Spirit's fire. Grumbling believers are spiritual fire extinguishers. They put out the Spirit's fire.

Because the Word of God commands that praise and thanksgiving be offered always, in all circumstances and for everything to God the Father in the name of the Lord Jesus, we conclude that any time when a believer is not giving thanks is sinning time. We also conclude that any circumstance in which a believer is not giving thanks is sinning circumstance.

The thought may arise in some hearts as to how they can really give thanks in all circumstances. Yes, the question may be arising in your own heart as to how you can give thanks in all things. Well, I want to confess that I cannot explain it all. I do not even have the responsibility to explain it. I only have the privilege to say that the Word of God says so and that saying so is final. That Word says that thanksgiving is to be offered to the Lord in ALL CIRCUMSTANCES for EVERYTHING.

This meaning that Praise and Thanksgiving are to be offered to God the Father in the name of Jesus Christ in ALL CIRCUMSTANCES EXCEPT NONE and in EVERYTHING EXCEPT NONE.

The Bible says that this giving of thanks to God the Father in the name of the Lord Jesus Christ is the will of God for every believer. If it is the will of God for every believer, then every believer is called to obey and not to rationalize. Every believer is called to obey and give thanks to the Father in every circumstance and for everything in the name of the Lord Jesus, before he has understood the reasoning behind it all. As he begins to obey before he has fully understood, God will give him light to understand more and more.

We are dealing with the Word of God. We are dealing with the thoughts of God. The thoughts of men are either logical or illogical. However, the thoughts of God are super logical. Because they are beyond human logic, they should be obeyed, even if they appear illogical at the beginning. God has not left it to us to choose in what circumstances we are to praise and thank Him. He knows that if He left it to us, we would have problems with our minds. So He has commanded us to give thanks for everything and in every circumstance. He has thus called us to move out of the human plane in which things are either logical or illogical into His plane in which the super rational operates. We are called to obey knowing fully well that, because it is His will, it is right before Him, obligatory to us and good for us! Begin to obey today!

When you miss the bus, praise Him. Also praise Him when the following take place:

1. Your money is stolen.
2. The plate is broken.
3. You are insulted.
4. A friend betrays you.
5. Your sleep is interrupted.
6. You receive an annoying letter.
7. Your inferior is promoted instead of you.
8. Your salary is reduced.
9. Your salary is not paid.
10. Thieves have broken into your house.
11. Your child has been involved in an accident.
12. The job you very much wanted has been given to someone else.
13. The electricity bill is higher than usual.
14. You missed your plane.
15. Etc.

You are under obligation to give thanks to God the Father in the name of Jesus in all circumstances and for everything. This is the unchanging will of God. Execute it, and may the Lord bless you exceedingly!

REMEMBER

You must thank the Lord for past events. You must thank Him for the most blessed events, the most heart lifting, and the most encouraging things that ever happened to you.

You must also thank the Lord for the most tragic, humiliating, painful, and the most discouraging events of your past life. God deserves praise for all and He must receive praise for everything.

17. PRAISE AND THANKSGIVING TO OUR SOVEREIGN LORD   1

The Lord God is our God. He is our sovereign Lord. He is Lord of all. He is Lord in all. He is sovereign. His purposes are excellent and He will accomplish all of them.

The Bible says:

> "Sing joyfully to the Lord, you righteous;
> it is fitting for the upright to praise him.
> Praise the Lord with the harp;
> make music to him on the ten stringed lyre.
> Sing to him a new song;
> play skilfully, and shout for joy.
> For the word of the Lord is right and true;

he is faithful in all he does.
The Lord loves righteousness and justice;
the earth is full of his unfailing love.
By the word of the Lord were the heaven's made,
their starry host by the breath of his mouth.
He gathers the waters of the sea into jars;
he puts the deep into storehouses.
Let all the earth fear the Lord;
let all the people of the world revere him.
<u>For he spoke and it came to be;</u>
<u>he commanded and it stood firm.</u>
<u>The Lord foils the plans of the nations;</u>
<u>he thwarts the purposes of the peoples.</u>
<u>But the plans of the Lord stand firm for ever,</u>
<u>the purposes of his heart through all generations</u>"
(Psalm 33:1 11).

Our God is sovereign in all the affairs of men. Everything that happens, happens either in His perfect will or in His permissive will. All that happens in His perfect will is just wonderful. It will exalt His holy name and bless man. All that happens in His permissive will will ultimately exalt His name and bless those who love Him. He has purposed to exalt His holy name, and no one can stop Him. He has purposed to bless those who love Him, and nothing can stop Him. The Bible says: «But he is unchangeable and who can turn him? What he desires, that he does. For he will complete what he appoints for me; and many such things are in mind. Therefore I am terrified at his presence; when I consider, I am in dread of him» (Job 23:13 15 RSV).

The Bible does not say, «He can complete what he appoints for me,» but «He will complete what he appoints for me.» Because He will complete what He has appointed concerning you, you should be at rest and minister Praise and Thanksgiving to Him in all circumstances and for everything.

The Bible again says, «I know that thou canst do all things, and that no purpose of thine can be thwarted» (Job 42:2 RSV). Yes, God can do all things. None of His purposes can be thwarted. There is not one purpose of God that can be thwarted! God cannot mean it to be B and it becomes C!! There is not one purpose of God that can be thwarted by man. There is not one purpose of God that can be thwarted by the devil.

The Bible says, «Many are the plans in a man's heart, but it is the Lord's purpose that prevails»(Proverbs 19:21). Yes, there are plans in the heart of man. There are plans in all directions. Some plans are to the left,
- to the right,
- forward,
- backward,
- upwards,
- downwards.

Yes, all these plans are there, but it is the purpose of the

Lord that prevails! Yes, the purpose of the Lord will prevail. The purpose of the Lord prevails, and because it will prevail and it prevails, praise and thanksgiving should go up to Him for everything, in all circumstances, at all times. This is the duty of man.

The Bible says,

> «The Lord Almighty has sworn, 'Surely, as I have planned, so it will be, and as I have purposed, so it will stand' «(Isaiah 14:24).

> «This is the plan determined for the whole world; this is the hand stretched out over all nations. For the Lord Almighty has purposed, and who can thwart him? His hand is stretched out, and who can turn it back?» (Isaiah 14:26 27).

> As God has planned, so it will be!
> As God has purposed, so it will stand!
> Who can thwart what God has purposed?
> Who can turn back His outstretched hand?

Because what He has planned must be; because what He has purposed will stand; because none can thwart what He has purposed; because none can turn back His outstretched hand, praise and thanksgiving should flow forth unceasingly to Him in everything, in all circumstances and at all times.

The Bible says,

> «I, even I, am the Lord,
>   and apart from me there is no saviour.
> I have revealed and saved and proclaimed
> I, and not some foreign god among you.
> You are my witnesses,» declares the Lord, «that I am God.
> Yes, and from ancient days I am he.
> No one can deliver out of my hand.
> When I act, who can reverse it?"
>   (Isaiah 43:11 13).

Because no one can reverse what the Lord does, praise and thanksgiving ought to go up to Him for His irreversible acts. Yes, praise and thanksgiving ought to go up to Him for each of His irreversible acts.

The Bible again says,

> «Remember this, fix it in mind,
> take it to heart, you rebels.
> Remember the former things, those of long ago;
> I am God, and there is no other;
> I am God, and there is none like me.
> I make known the end from the beginning,
> from ancient times, what is still to come.
> I say: My purpose will stand, and I will do all
> that I please.
> From the east I summon a bird of prey;

from a far off land, a man to fulfil my purpose.
What I have said, that will I bring about;
what I have planned, that will I do»
(Isaiah 46:8 11).

Do you take note of the authority of God that is being manifested? Do you perceive His might?

My purpose will stand!
I will do all that I please!!
From the east I summon a bird of prey!!!
From a far off land I summon a man
to fulfil my purpose!!!!
What I have said, that I will bring about!!!!!
What I have planned, that I will do!!!!!!

This ought to make you and me fall before Him and worship Him, saying, «Great and marvellous are your deeds, Lord God Almighty. Just and true are your ways, King of the ages» (Revelation 15:3).

The Bible continues to press home the sovereignty of God, saying, «Men of Israel, listen to this: Jesus of Nazareth was a man accredited by God to you by miracles, wonders and signs, which God did among you through him, as you yourselves know. This man was handed over to you by God's set purpose and foreknowledge; and you, with the help of wicked men put him to death by nailing him to the cross. But God raised him from the dead, freeing him from the agony of death, because it was impossible for death to keep its hold on him» (Acts 2:22 24).

The Bible says that Jesus was handed over to the Jewish leaders and authorities by God's set purpose! With God's foreknowledge!! It was a set purpose. It was a purpose that no one could frustrate. That set purpose determined that He would be crucified between two thieves; that set purpose established that He would be given vinegar to drink; that set purpose established that He would be raised from the dead and that set purpose came to pass in every detail without fail. Because it was so, praise and thanksgiving ought to be given to the Lord God in all circumstances, at all times and for everything!

The Bible says, «For truly in this city there were gathered together against thy holy servant Jesus, whom thou didst anoint, both Herod and Pontius Pilate, with the Gentiles and the peoples of Israel, to do whatever thy hand had predestined to take place» (Acts 4:27 28 RSV).

Who were gathered together in Jerusalem against the Lord Jesus? The Bible says: «Pontius Pilate, the Gentiles and the people of Israel.» There were three different groups. They had three different backgrounds. However, these differences were ignored as they came together. Their motives were different but all the same, they came together. What did they come together for? The Bible says, «TO DO WHATEVER THY HAND HAD PREDETERMINED TO TAKE PLACE.»

This is not to say that they wanted to do God's will. No! They wanted to execute the desires of their hearts. They wanted to oppose God. They wanted to frustrate the purpose of God. But in all their attempts, they only accomplished one thing they accomplished the will of God. They accomplished what God had predetermined would take place. They brought God's will to pass.

If God rules in the affairs of men; if God will accomplish all His purpose; if His hand cannot be stopped; if the horse is made ready for battle but the victory belongs to the Lord, then the believer who walks in the will of God has nothing to fear. The believer who walks in the will of God has nothing to worry about. The believer who walks in the will of God should come to perfect rest; the believer who walks in the will of God needs to thank the Lord in all circumstances, for everything and in everything, because God is ruling in all circumstances, in everything and in every way.

> History then becomes, no longer an accident or the design of man, but the unfolding of the plan of God. History then becomes, not an accident, but the unfolding of God's predetermined plan - a plan that must come to pass. History - the history of an individual,
> - a family
> - a group of individuals,
> - cities,
> - nations and
> - continents,

then becomes the unfolding of God's will,

bringing of God's will to pass,
execution of God's will.

It could be that that will, that will of God, is judgment or
mercy, but it is God's will. It is no accident. God raises
up and God brings down; God promotes and God demotes.
Glory be to His all-Holy Name! Amen.

18. PRAISE AND THANKSGIVING TO OUR SOVEREIGN LORD 2. THE EXAMPLE OF JOB.

Many believers believe and act as if they were victims of
man or victims of circumstances. Many more believe that
they are victims of the devil. The truth is that the believer
is not the victim of man! The believer is not the victim
of circumstances. The believer is not the victim of the
devil. The Lord reigns in the believer's circumstances. The
Lord reigns over the devil. Many believers see the devil in
everything. Many see the devil from morning until evening,
and many proclaim his name unceasingly. Unfortunately,
for many believers, the devil is more real than God. This
ought not to be so. One man of God said, «I refuse to deal
with secondary causes. I deal with God. He is my Father
and He reigns. Unless He allows a thing, it will not happen
to me. He may allow it in His perfect will or He may allow
it in His permissive will. Whether it is His perfect will or

His permissive will, nothing but His best can be allowed to come to me. I am at rest in Him.»

The Bible says, «One day the sons of God came to present themselves before the Lord, and Satan also came with them. The Lord said to Satan, 'Where have you come from?' Satan answered the Lord, 'From roaming through the earth and going to and fro in it.' Then the Lord said to Satan, 'Have you considered my servant Job? There is no one on earth like him; he is blameless and upright, a man who fears God and shuns evil.' 'Does Job fear God for nothing?' Satan replied. 'Have you not put a hedge around him and his household and everything he has? You have blessed the work of his hands, so that his flocks and herds are spread throughout the land. But stretch out your hand and strike everything he has, and he will surely curse you to your face' « (Job 1:6 12).

Many of us would want to see the devil here and the devil there. The Bible puts God in the central position. It says, «One day the sons of God came to present themselves before the Lord, and Satan also came.» If God is God; if He is omnipotent, omnipresent, and omniscient, then we are sure that God knew that Satan would attend that meeting. If He had wanted him not to come, He would have stopped him; for God is able to stop anything and everything that the devil would want to do.

God was the One who engaged the devil in the conversation. Before the Lord started the conversation, He knew from

start to finish where it would end. He knew beforehand
what the devil would say. He knew what He was doing and
He knew to whom He was talking. It was the Lord God
who brought Job into the scene, and before He brought him
in He knew where that conversation would lead to. Satan
answered back to God to explain away Job's faithfulness,
righteousness and integrity. This could not have happened
without God's permission.

Satan said, «Have you not put a hedge around him and his
household and everything he has?» He was saying, «I would
have attacked him, but I cannot attack him because the
hedge that You have put around him is in the way.» God put
the hedge! Satan could not break through while the hedge
was on. Satan suggested that if the hedge were removed, he
would go into action and things would be different and the
reaction of Job different.

God decided to permit Satan to attack Job. He decided to
withdraw the hedge in a limited way. The Bible says, «The
Lord said to Satan, «Very well, then, everything he has is
in your hands, but on the man himself do not lay a finger»
(Job 1:12). As is obvious, God was absolutely in control.
Everything was determined by Him.

Satan left God's presence with permission to have authority
over all that Job had. However, he was forbidden to touch
Job's life. He went from God's presence and set things in
motion. The following were the results of what he did. The

Bible says, «One day when Job's sons and daughters were feasting and drinking wine at their oldest brother's house, a messenger came to Job and said, 'The oxen were ploughing and the donkeys were grazing nearby and the Sabeans attacked and carried them off. They put the servants to the sword, and I am the only one who has escaped to tell you!'

While he was still speaking, another messenger came and said, 'The fire of God fell from the sky and burned up the sheep and the servants, and I am the only one who has escaped to tell you!'

While he was still speaking, another messenger came and said, 'The Chaldeans formed three raiding parties and swept down on your camels and carried them off. They put the servants to the sword, and I am the only one who has escaped to tell you!'

While he was still speaking, yet another messenger came and said, 'Your sons and daughters were feasting and drinking wine at their oldest brother's house, when suddenly a mighty wind swept in from the desert and struck the four corners of the house. It collapsed on them and they are dead, and I am the only one who has escaped to tell you!' «(Job 1:13 19).

All these were activities of Satan. However, he received permission from the Lord God to carry them out. God could have stopped each one of them, but in His higher purpose for Job, He stopped none of them.

How did Job react? The Bible says, «At this, Job got up and tore his robe and shaved his head. Then he fell to the ground in worship and said:

> «Naked I came from my mother's womb,
> and naked I shall depart.
> The Lord gave and the Lord has taken away; may the name of the Lord be praised"   (Job 1:20 21).

There are three great truths here that could transform any life. The first one is that the best thing to do when the darkest moment seems to have come upon you is to fall down to the ground and worship. Such worship is an act of greatest surrender. It is an act of the greatest confession of the sovereignty of God. It is the greatest thing that anyone could do. It honours God and testifies to deep spiritual maturity.

The second is that each one comes naked from his mother's womb and each one departs empty handed out of this world. The worry about this thing and that thing is uncalled for. The accumulation of things that cannot be taken along when the time comes to leave this world is folly. Wise people send their things to heaven ahead of time, by investing them in the winning of the lost for Christ and in the building of the saints for Christ.

The third thing that is evident in the confession of Job is that he considered himself as dealing with God and not with the devil. He did not say, «The Lord gave and the devil has taken away.» He did say, «The Lord gave and the Lord has taken away,» because of ignorance of the part the devil might have played. He knew that God was sovereign and in control and had allowed it all for his best interest. Therefore, he praised the name of the Lord!

Job was afflicted, but in the end his knowledge of God was perfected and he had twice what he had lost. The Bible says,

> «Then Job replied to the Lord:
> ... My ears have heard of you
> but now my eyes have seen you.
> Therefore I despise myself
> and repent in dust and ashes»
>   (Job 42:1 6).

Job ended up earning a broken and contrite heart. This was more precious to God than his pre affliction righteousness. He loved the Lord before he was afflicted, but after the affliction, he had something that is most precious to God a broken and a contrite heart. The Psalmist said, «My sacrifice O God, is a broken spirit; a broken and contrite heart, O God, you will not despise» (Psalm 51:17 NIV). To have a broken and contrite heart as one's sacrifice is evidence of great spirituality. God wants to bring each one of us there. Let us allow Him to have His way. Let us praise and thank Him for the method, the timing and the circumstances through which He has chosen to accomplish this great purpose, and we shall be blessed indeed.

At the material level, the Bible says, «After Job had prayed for his friends, the Lord made him prosperous again and gave him twice as much as he had before. All his brothers and sisters and everyone who had known him before came and ate with him in his house. They comforted and consoled him over all the trouble the Lord had brought upon him, and each one gave him a piece of silver and a gold ring. The Lord blessed the latter part of Job's life more than the first. He had fourteen thousand sheep, six thousand camels, and a thousand yoke of oxen and a thousand donkeys. And he also had seven sons and three daughters. The first daughter he named Jemimah, the second Keziah and the third Keren Happuch. Nowhere in all the land were there found women as beautiful as Job's daughters, and their father granted them an inheritance along with their brothers. After this, Job lived a hundred and forty years; he saw his children and their children to the fourth generation. And so he died, old and full of years» (Job 42:10 17).

Praise the Lord!
Praise the Lord!
Praise the Lord!

19. THE LORD JESUS' PRACTICE OF PRAISE AND THANKSGIVING AS A SACRIFICE

Our blessed Saviour, the Lord Jesus, practised offering praise and thanksgiving as a sacrifice. He is our example and we should follow Him and imitate Him.

The Bible says, «Then Jesus began to denounce the cities in which most of his miracles had been performed, because they did not repent. 'Woe to you, Korazin! Woe to you, Bethsaida!

If the miracles that were performed in you had been performed in Tyre and Sidon, they would have repented long ago in sackcloth and ashes. But I tell you, it will be more bearable for Tyre and Sidon on the day of judgment than for you. And you, Capernaum, will you be lifted up to the skies? No, you will go down to the depths. If the miracles that were performed in you had been performed in Sodom, it would have remained to this day. But I tell you that it will be more bearable for Sodom on the day of judgment than for you.'

At that time Jesus said, 'I praise you, Father, Lord of heaven and earth, because you have hidden these things from the wise and learned, and revealed them to little children. Yes, Father, for this was your good pleasure' « (Matthew 11:20 26).

The Lord had performed many mighty signs, wonders and miracles in Korazin,

> Bethsaida, and
>
> Capernaum

and these miracles were meant to lead these cities to repentance. The people in these cities saw the mighty works of the Lord but did not repent.

From a human perspective, it was a low moment for the Lord Jesus. It was a moment when He faced the fact of the hardness of human hearts. It was a moment when He faced the reality of being rejected. What did He do? He could have gone away in sorrow and not turned to His Father. He could have questioned the Father as to why He did not cause them to believe. He could have been discouraged. However, the Lord Jesus did not do any of these. He simply turned to His Father and offered the sacrifice of praise, saying, «I praise you, Father, Lord of heaven and earth, because you have hidden these things from the wise and learned, and revealed them to little children. Yes, Father, for this was your good pleasure.»

God always acts in His good pleasure; and for each such act, praise and thanksgiving should be given to Him.

The Lord Jesus did that and left us an example that we should follow in His steps.

You, go and do likewise!

20. EXAMPLE OF DIFFICULT CIRCUMSTANCES UNDER WHICH COSTLY PRAISE MUST FLOW FORTH TO OUR SOVEREIGN LORD AND GOD.

1. When you fail an examination, the failure might have been permitted by the Lord so that the following good may come onto you and so make you more like Jesus:

a. To humble your proud heart and help you to become humble, since God resists the proud of heart. All that will help a proud person to become humble is good for the person.

b. To save you from trouble. Because you failed the examination, you might have to repeat a class. This means that you cannot go abroad as soon as you would have gone. This delay means that you might have been protected from a fatal accident, or from meeting someone to whom you might have been emotionally attracted to your ruin, or from being taught by people who would have ruined your faith and caused you to backslide.

c. To cause you to meet someone you would not have met, and whom meeting would help you to know the Lord more, love Him more and serve Him more.

d. To cause you to see that you were lazy, repent

of it and put on the spirit of hard work which will revolutionize the rest of your life and bring you to a top position academically whereas, had you had an average pass, you would have gone on to be an average person for the rest of your life.

e. To cause you to lead someone to the Lord, while repeating your class, who will one day bless your ministry in an exceptional way or who will one day become your life partner.

f. To cause you to become understanding with people who work very hard and fail, and thus develop a ministry of compassion to those who are suffering from one hardship or another.

g. To cause you to see that the glory of this world is no glory at all, and then to begin to seek the glory that comes from above.

h. To cause you to bring the Lord Jesus into your studies. It could be that before you failed the examination, you had confidence in your own intelligence. The failure has made you realize that your own intelligence will fail you. You, therefore, need God given intelligence. You, therefore, ask the Lord Jesus for wisdom and, by so doing, lean on Him for everything in all of the future. This is worth any price paid.

2. When your father, mother, brother, son or daughter dies after believing in the Lord. This death has been permitted by the Lord for one of the following reasons or for another reason which we are not going to cite, but which is for the best interest of the person and those of his who love the Lord Jesus and are called according to His purpose. This death will cause the person and his to be like Jesus in that the following blessings are in store:

a. The Lord has seen that the person has attained his maximum spiritual height and that it is good for him to go and meet his Lord at that level, so as to receive the best reward from the Lord.

b. The person has developed well spiritually, but as the Lord looked into the future, He saw that if he continued to live, he would backslide and fall into temptation and either ruin his spiritual life completely or mar it extensively. In order not to have the person suffer such loss, the Lord took him away so as to save him from spiritual harm.

c. The Lord saw that if the person continued to live, he would catch an incurable disease that would cause him untold pain and trouble, with no real spiritual advantages. In order to save him from such agony, the Lord took him to Himself to spare him pain for his own good.

d. The Lord saw that if he continued to live, he would fall into sin that would ruin his family and all those who love him. In order to save his family from ruin, the Lord decided to take him to Himself, instead of allowing him to continue to live and so ruin the family.

e. The Lord saw that if he continued to live, he might become sick with an incurable disease that would drain family funds, love and care and leave a crushing burden on multitudes in the family, who will each not be able to fulfil the call of God on their lives. Take, for example, a father who is blind, deaf and paralysed in the legs and who stays in this condition for forty years. It could mean that the ministries and careers of the people of that home are altered and damaged beyond measure, since the family will know drain in all areas for those forty years! Because the Lord saw this, he decided to take the person home to Himself.

f. The Lord saw that if the person continued to live, he might oppose a marriage of one member of the family (a marriage that is very much in the centre of God's will) and that this would lead to a marriage outside the will of God that would leave disastrous results for generations. Out of love for the family up to the third and forth generation, the Lord decided to save the situation by taking him to Himself. This can only be a good death for which the Lord should receive praise and thanksgiving.

g. The Lord saw that if he continued to live, he would depart from the Lord and originate a Godless, Christless religion, which would spread and cause many to go to the lake of fire. God, out of His love for multitudes, took him in order to save him and all whom he would have led astray.

1. When...
2. Your car is stolen.
3. Your car is hit by another.
4. Your car is involved in an accident that will take money to repair.
5. Your house catches fire.
6. Your car catches fire and burns to ashes.
7. Your friend betrays you.
8. Your certificates are lost.
9. Your bank goes bankrupt.
10. There is drought in your country.
11. There is a plague in your city.
12. Your boss is immoral.
13. Your boss is a thief.
14. Your boss hates you.
15. Your boss prefers another to you.
16. Your boss always gives you more work than he gives to others and yet he does not compensate you for it.
17. The police want a bribe from you.
18. The government is corrupt.

19. The government is dishonest.
20. The government lacks vision.
21. There is a shortage of jobs.
22. Salaries have been decreased.
23. The currency has been threatened with devaluation.
24. The currency has been devalued.
25. You are told that you have cancer.
26. You are told that your son has AIDS.
27. You are told that your wife will never conceive.
28. You are told that you are sterile.
29. You are told that you have been thrown out of your job.
30. You have been involved in a train accident.
31. The food has got burnt.
32. The lights have failed.
33. The gas runs out just as you are half way through with the cooking.
34. Your shirt has been destroyed in the process of ironing.
35. Your last coins are stolen.
36. Your note books have been stolen or lost one week to the final examination.
37. Your daughter has fallen to the ground with the food she was bringing to you, and she has bruises.
38. You have lost your keys.
39. Your wife has misplaced your keys and you are almost late for work.
40. Your husband has run away with another woman.
41. Your wife has run away with another man.
42. Your husband has brought in another woman as a second wife.
43. Your husband has been caught in the act of stealing.

44. Your child has stolen your money.
45. Your child has stolen money from someone else.
46. Your secretary has typed your name wrongly.
47. A neighbour's cattle have broken into your maize farm and are grazing in it.
48. Your wife disobeys you.
49. Your wife insults you.
50. Your husband tells you that you are ugly.
51. Your husband tells you that he has found another woman who is better than you.
52. Your baby is born deformed.
53. An unbeliever dies.

Why and how can one honestly thank God for the death of an unbeliever? Well, the Lord says that we should give thanks in everything and in all circumstances. This must include this one. What good can come out of the death of an unbeliever for himself and for those who are his? Why did God permit it and why should He be thanked for it? Below are some good things that could result from the death of an unbeliever:

a. The unbeliever might have hardened his heart to the point where God had given him up. So with respect to salvation, there is no hope for him, even if he were to live for another one hundred years. Having lost all the opportunities offered him to believe, the benefits that come from his death must be seen from another perspective and not from that of his own salvation.

b. His unbelief might have provoked God to judge him most severely, so that he might be plagued with an incurable disease. This would have meant that he would have started suffering in this life and to continue to suffer in the lake of fire. God, out of mercy and love for him, decided to let him die in order to avoid the physical suffering in this life. God should be thanked for that act of sparing him physical suffering.

c. His unbelief might have led to the unbelief of one or more people. The Lord, therefore, out of love for those people, decided to remove the one who would have caused them to fall out of the way. The Lord should be thanked for that death that opened the way for the salvation of others.

d. He might have fallen sick with a dreadful disease that would have changed the course of many lives that are associated with him - change that would have been disastrous. God, out of love for the man's people, decided that he should die before he ever became a problem. He should be thanked for that.

54. Someone curses you. When someone curses you, you should, in that circumstance, give thanks to the Lord for everything. David saw this clearly. The Bible says, «As King David approached Bahurim, a man from the same clan as

Saul's family came out from there. His name was Shimei son of Gera, and he cursed as he came out. He pelted David and all the King's officials with stones, though all the troops and the special guard were on David's right and left. As he cursed, Shimei said, 'Get out, get out, you man of blood, you scoundrel! The Lord has repaid you for all the blood that you shed in the household of Saul, in whose place you have reigned. The Lord has handed the kingdom over to your son Absalom. You have come to ruin because you are a man of blood!' Then Abishai son of Zeruiah said to the king, 'Why should this dead dog curse my lord the king? Let me go over and cut off his head.' But the king said, 'What do you and I have in common, you sons of Zeruiah? If he is cursing because the Lord said to him, 'Curse David,' who can ask, 'Why do you do this?' David then said to Abishai and all his officials, 'My son, who is my own flesh, is trying to take my life. How much more, then, this Benjaminite! Leave him alone; let him curse, for the Lord has told him to. It may be that the Lord will see my distress and repay me with good for the cursing I am receiving today.'

So David and his men continued along the road while Shimei was going along the hillside opposite him, cursing as he went and throwing stones at him and showering him with dirt. The king and all the people with him arrived at their destination exhausted. And there he refreshed himself» (2 Samuel 16:5 14).

PART FIVE

THE PRACTICE
OF PRAISE

THE MINISTRY OF PRAISE AND THANKSGIVING

21. RECORDING THE DETAILS OF YOUR LIFE WITH PRAISE AND THANKSGIVING IN VIEW

A person cannot wait to thank the Lord just for the great events of his life. God is to be thanked for each event of life. Without each of these events, you might not have become the person you are today.

Some time ago, I took some time to thank the Lord for the events of my life that were plain and ordinary, but that had contributed to making me the person I am today. Below is the list. I suggest that you should make yours. After you have made it, take time to thank the Lord for each event.

I have decided to share here just the first 100 items of praise that I wrote for the earliest part of my life (the period between 0 & 9 years as I could remember them at the age of 41). As for you, write out such events for your whole life and share with those who love you. To prepare for praising and thanking God in the future, keep a record of five or ten items of praise and thanksgiving daily. You will soon have an excellent record of God's deeds in your life to thank Him for. This is your wealth items of praise and thanksgiving.

1. Lord, thank You that You decided to create me from the foundations of the world.
2. Lord, thank You that You also decided to create me and ordain me unto eternal life.

3. Lord, thank You for choosing Solomon Fomum Tanee to be my father.
4. Lord, thank You for choosing Rebecca Angum Tanee to be my mother.
5. Lord, thank You for deciding that I should be born in Africa.
6. Lord, thank You for deciding that I should be born in Cameroon.
7. Lord, thank You for deciding that I should be born in the North West Province.
8. Lord, thank You for deciding that I should be born in Momo Division.
9. Lord, thank You for deciding that I should be born in the Widikum Tribe.
10. Lord, thank You for deciding that I should be born in Moghamo.
11. Lord, thank You for deciding that I should be born in Effah village.
12. Lord, thank You for predetermining that I should be born in Atuaku.
13. Lord, thank You for predetermining that I should be the third child of the family.
14. Lord, thank You for predetermining that I should be the second son of the family.
15. Lord, thank You for deciding that Peter Akum Fomum should be my elder brother.
16. Lord, thank You for deciding that Mary Uko Mbafor should be my elder sister.
17. Lord, thank You for deciding and overruling that my

parents should have six children.

18. Lord, thank You for deciding and overruling that of the six children, four should be boys and two girls.

19. Lord, thank You for predetermining that Hodia Ngomwi Fon should be my immediate younger sister.

20. Lord, thank You for predetermining that Calvin Atud Fomum should be my younger brother.

21. Lord, thank You for predetermining that Emmanuel Mbah Fomum should be my youngest brother.

22. Lord, thank You for the fact that You caused me to be born in Wumnembug.

23. Lord, thank You for granting that the first five years of my life should be spent there.

24. Lord, thank You for that day when I saw Hodia born.

25. Lord, thank You for Ndah who was my childhood friend.

26. Lord, thank You for Fobang who was another friend.

27. Lord, thank You for that day when Ndah and I cooked plantains.

28. Lord, thank You for causing my father to be selected for further training.

29. Lord, thank You for the journey to Bafut.

30. Lord, thank You for that one year spent in Bafut.

31. Lord, thank You for that period when Mummy was taken to Banso Hospital for treatment.

32. Lord, thank You for the care that Ni Peter took of me during that time.

33. Lord, thank You for that pair of shoes that he tried to mend so that I could have shoes.

34. Lord, thank You for all the other children in that compound.
35. Lord, thank You for the house in which we lived then.
36. Lord, thank You for that journey to Moghamo in 1951.
37. Lord, thank You for that visit to Njimbein.
38. Lord, thank You for that stay at Fon Buroro's.
39. Lord, thank You for the kindness of my late cousin, Moses.
40. Lord, thank You for the journey to Nyasoso.
41. Lord, thank You for that day when I first went to Primary School in April 1952.
42. Lord, thank You for my teacher Mr Asale.
43. Lord, thank You for that first day when I was taught A and B and which I found difficult to remember.
44. Lord, thank You for causing me to be the 5th during my first term in Primary School, even though I went to school in April instead of January.
45. Lord, thank You for the present of a bag that my Daddy gave me to congratulate and encourage me.
46. Lord, thank You for granting that I be the first at the end of my first year in Primary School.
47. Lord, thank You for granting that I should be able to read the Douala premier in Infants One.
48. Lord, thank You for Mr. Esome whom You appointed to teach me in Infants Two.
49. Lord, thank You for the special love that You gave him for me.
50. Lord, thank You for the opportunity to go and teach the premier to Infants One pupils during reading

classes for Infants Two since I had completed the book very well.

51. Lord, thank You for the special love that You put into Mr Esome's heart for me, so that he taught me additional things.

52. Lord, thank You for those occasions when I was called to solve problems in Standard One which Standard One pupils could not solve.

53. Lord, thank You for the day I had three sums wrong and some had all and I felt very humiliated.

54. Lord, thank You for that day when I was asked not to come back unless my clothes were washed and I could not understand why.

55. Lord, thank You for that day when I said the «twelve times table», which a Standard Four boy could not say and I was given three pennies as a gift by a teacher.

56. Lord, thank You for that examination during which I scored 598 marks out of 600.

57. Lord, thank You for sending Lambert to Nyasoso in 1953 and for the challenge that he brought.

58. Lord, thank You for Jean Yatchi and the challenge that he too brought.

59. Lord, thank You for that day when Lambert and I nearly fought, after which we became friends.

60. Lord, thank You for the academic atmosphere of the school compound.

61. Lord, thank You for the farm to which we went regularly.

62. Lord, thank You for the abundant oranges on the

mission compound.

63. Lord, thank You for the abundant grapefruits on the mission compound.
64. Lord, thank You for the abundant guavas.
65. Lord, thank You for the evening competitions.
66. Lord, thank You for the first term in Standard One when I was first.
67. Lord, thank You for that day when I could recite the "twelve times table".
68. Lord, thank You for giving me the first place in class during the second term in Standard One.
69. Lord, thank You for my brilliant performance at Sunday School.
70. Lord, thank You for that day when I went with Daddy for the sharing of that monkey meat among the pastors in training.
71. Lord, thank You for that day when we harvested so many oranges that we made orange drinks from them on the farm.
72. Lord, thank You for that day when Ma Mary and I went fishing and I caught nothing.
73. Lord, thank You for that day when we harvested so many cocoyams that we buried some in the ground in the bush.
74. Lord, thank You for that memorable day when Nini Peter was on the farm hoeing and Mummy and Ma Mary were there, and Mummy hissed to Ni Peter in the vernacular.
75. Lord, thank You for that day when we were carrying

sand for money and, because I was boasting, I separated my sand from Ma Mary's, worked so hard and in the end proved beyond all doubt to myself that she had contributed far more than myself in the collection of the preceding day.

76. Lord, thank You for the day on which Calvin was born and I was sent to Ndimjoh for oil.

77. Lord, thank You for that day when we went to carry plantains from Ndimjoh with Ma Mary and Samson Beteke.

78. Lord, thank You for the day when Christopher Fai, other boys and myself went to pray in the chapel that is near the road at Nyasoso.

79. Lord, thank You for that day when we were beaten by Mwakole Juniors and I ran out of the goal area in fear of the rings that they were wearing.

80. Lord, thank You for that day when Thaddeus Bonkam stole the sugar canes and the young people gathered to eat them, and You gave me the courage not to eat them.

81. Lord, thank You for the cowardice that caused me to swear that I would never tell the fact that the sugar canes were stolen.

82. Lord, thank You for that day when Ma Mary and I went to Tombel and back on Saturday, a distance of 29 kilometres, when I was less than ten years old.

83. Lord, thank You for the excellent Sunday School Teachers that You gave me.

84. Lord, thank You for the stories that they told me

about You that were imprinted indelibly on my mind.

85. Lord, thank You for those occasions when Daddy, Ni Peter and I had to go and cut grass on farms during holidays in order to have money.

86. Lord, thank You for Mummy who always fed us well.

87. Lord, thank You for the gift of selling 'akra.'

88. Lord, thank You for the fact that You enabled me to sell 'akra' for all those years without ever stealing one or eating one without permission.

89. Lord, thank You for protecting my money so that it was never stolen.

90. Lord, thank You for enabling me to sell groundnuts without eating even one grain, day by day, for over a two year period between the ages of eight and ten.

91. Lord, thank You for protecting my money that day when at the age of eight years, I sold the groundnuts, forgot the money at the site of selling and only remembered when I was nearing home.

92. Lord, thank You for those honest men who picked up the money and kept it for me, so that when I came back to look for it, they gave it to me.

93. Lord, thank You for that night when Christopher Fai and I went to the Chapel to pray at midnight and got so frightened by some noise, but nevertheless clung to the altar and prayed.

94. Lord, thank You for that event which took place when I privately went and asked to work on the coffee farm of that man in Mwakole. Thank You, Lord, for the portion he gave me to clear for money. Thank you

for enabling me to invest my private hours there and to work secretly. Thank You, Lord, for that day when I was paid two shillings for the work I had done and I joyously brought the two shillings and gave Daddy to his utter amazement, at the age of eight.

95. Lord, thank You for the look I saw on his face that day that made me think that he was saying, «I am proud of you.»

96. Thank You, Lord, for that period when I was so proud that Rev. Fai gave Jean Yatsi some money so that he would outclass me in the coming examination, so as to silence my pride.

97. Thank You, Lord, that You enabled him to outclass me the next term for the first time, and I felt deeply humiliated and wept for sorrow.

98. Thank You, Lord, for the training I received such that from the age of six, I had to wake up at 3.30 a.m. daily.

99. Thank You, Lord, for Ni Peter's interest in me that caused him to force me to do private competitive examinations with boys who were one class ahead of me, and when I was not first, he beat me.

100. Thank You, Lord, for my darling father who worked so hard at the seminary, often putting his legs in a bucket of cold water so as not to fall asleep, and the impact of this on my life.

22. PRAISING AND THANKING GOD FOR FUTURE EVENTS

If praising and thanking God for past and present events is a must, then the people of faith must also learn to thank the Lord for future events. The future is guaranteed by God, and His promises make the future certain.

The Apostle Paul gives the prescription, 'Do not be anxious about anything, but in everything, by prayer and petition, with thanksgiving, present your requests to God. And the peace of God, which transcends all understanding, will guard your hearts and your minds in Christ Jesus» (Philippians 4:6 7).

All that could become a cause for anxiety is to be brought to the Lord in prayer. Specific requests are to be made to the Father. Faith is to be exercised to believe that He has heard and granted the request. The genuineness of the faith is to be manifested by thanking the Lord for answers received, and while the answers to be received are being waited upon so that they might be manifest, faith is to flow forth in unceasing praise and thanksgiving. We outline these steps as follows:

1. Prayer is clearly made to the Father in the name of the Lord Jesus.

2. By faith the answer to prayer is received from the Father in the name of the Lord Jesus.

3. Praise and thanksgiving are given to the Father, in the name of the Lord Jesus, for the answer received by faith.

4. Praise and thanksgiving continue to be given to the Father in the name of the Lord Jesus for the answer received by faith, until faith gives way to sight.

5. Praise and thanksgiving continue to be given to the Father for that which has been received by faith and is manifest to sight.

Seen in this way, praise and thanksgiving are central in all praying. It is the absence of these elements that causes many not to receive what they ask. Many are able to ask with faith from the beginning, but afterwards they doubt and all is lost. Doubting easily comes in when the faith is not sustained and strengthened by praise and thanksgiving. Unfortunately, believers keep asking and asking until the asking gives birth to doubting. They ought to have asked and then moved over to praise and thanksgiving, and in that way their faith would have been strengthened until faith gave way to sight.

The Bible says of Abraham, «Against all hope, Abraham in hope believed and so became the father of many nations, just as it had been said to him, 'So shall your offspring be.' Without weakening in his faith, he faced the fact that his body was as good as dead -- since he was about a hundred years old   and that Sarah's womb was also dead. Yet he did not waver through unbelief regarding the promise of God, but was strengthened in his faith and gave glory to God, being fully persuaded that God had power to do what he had promised» (Romans 4:18 21).

The Revised Standard Version renders verse 20 as follows: «No distrust made him waver concerning the promise of God, but he grew strong in his faith as he gave glory to God.» YES, HE GREW STRONG IN HIS FAITH AS HE GAVE GLORY TO GOD.

Giving glory to God is the Ministry of Praise and Thanksgiving. It could be re written, «But he grew strong in his faith as he ministered Praise and Thanksgiving to the Lord.»

It becomes evident that while praise and thanksgiving flow forth to God the Father, growth in faith becomes the possession of the one who is praising and thanking the Lord.

The following proclamation to God from Jonah while he was still in the fish is thought provoking:

> «In my distress I called to the Lord,
> and he answered me.
> From the depth of the grave I called for help,
> and you listened to my cry.

You hurled me into the deep,
into the very heart of the seas,
and the current swirled about me;
all your waves and breakers swept over me.
I said, 'I have been banished from your sight;
yet I will look again towards your holy temple.'
The engulfing waters threatened me,
the deep was wrapped around my head;
To the roots of the mountains I sank down;
the earth beneath barred me in for ever.
But you brought my life up from the pit,
O Lord my God.
When my life was ebbing away,
I remembered you, Lord,
and my prayer rose to you,
to your holy temple.
Those who cling to worthless idols
forfeit the grace that could be theirs.
But I, with a song of thanksgiving,
will sacrifice to you.
What I have vowed I will make good.
Salvation comes from the Lord.'
And the Lord commanded the fish, and it vomited
Jonah unto dry land»
(Jonah 2:2 10).

Jonah prayed and believed the Lord. He believed that the
Lord had heard him. Even though he was physically still
in the fish, by faith he was already out. Consequently, his

prayer to the Lord was one of thanksgiving for something that had already happened and had been settled. He believed God and already saw himself out of the fish. What was settled in prayer was settled finally, and he was not moved by what he saw to continue to ask. He thanked the God who had delivered him.

Bear in mind that as to sight, Jonah was still in the fish. However, as to faith in answer to prayer, he was already out. Therefore he spoke to the Lord of what had already happened:

> I called to the Lord and he answered me.
> I called for help and you listened to my cry.
> You hurled me into the deep.
> Current swirled about me.
> Waves and breakers swept over me.

At the moment when he was confessing these things to the Lord, current still swirled about him and waves and breakers still swept over him in the visible. He ignored these and believed the word of deliverance that the Lord had given him, and confessed what the Lord had offered him and he had received by faith, and refused to confess what he was seeing with his physical eyes or feeling with his physical senses. He believed God's word instead of what he saw!

Praise and thanksgiving for future events is based upon the fact that God has promised us what will happen in the future and that we have believed Him and decided irrevocably to stake our future on His promises. We then water the faith by praise and thanksgiving while we wait for the future to become the present and for the things received by faith to become objects received by sight. We can present it as follows:

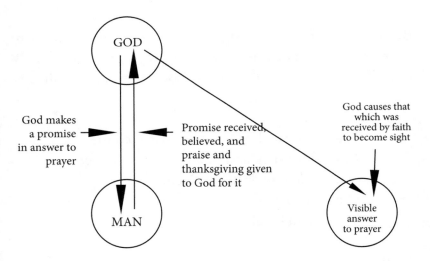

May we believe the Lord. May we ask and receive from Him. May we praise and thank Him for what He gave in the past. May we praise and thank Him for His unchanging faithfulness before we make our requests to Him. May we make our requests to Him in the name of the Lord Jesus. May we believe that we have received what we have asked for. May we then water our faith with unceasing praise and thanksgiving, and then our faith will become sight, and then may we continue to praise the Lord and to thank Him; for that is the best thing we can do to Him, to His cause and to ourselves. Amen.

24. PRAISE AND THANKSGIVING
IN HEAVEN

Some believers think that heaven will be a place for idleness. Nothing could be further from the truth. The book of Revelation enables us to have a glimpse of heaven. The Bible says:

«In the centre, around the throne, were four living creatures, and they were covered with eyes, in front and behind. The first living creature was like a lion, the second was like an ox, the third had a face like a man, the fourth was like a flying eagle. Each of the four living creatures had six wings and was covered with eyes all around, even under his wings. Day and night they never stop saying:

- 'Holy, holy, holy is
- the Lord God Almighty,
- who was, and is, and is to come.'

Whenever the living creatures give glory, honour and thanks to him who sits on the throne and who lives for ever and ever, the twenty four elders fall down before him who is on the throne, and worship him who lives for ever and ever. They lay their crowns before the throne and say:

'You are worthy, our Lord and God,
to receive glory and honour and power;

> for you created all things,
> and by your will they were created
> and have their being' « (Revelation 4:6 11).

The Bible again shows us another picture of heaven. «Then I saw a Lamb, looking as if it had been slain, standing in the centre of the throne, encircled by the four living creatures and the elders. He had seven horns and seven eyes, which are the seven spirits of God sent out into all the earth. He came and took the scroll from the right hand of him who sat on the throne. And when he had taken it, the four living creatures and the twenty four elders fell down before the Lamb. Each one had a harp and they were holding golden bowls full of incense, which are the prayers of the saints. And they sang a new song:

> 'You are worthy to take the scroll
> and to open its seals,
> because you were slain,
> and with your blood
> you purchased men for God
> from every tribe and language
> and people and nation.
> You have made them to be a kingdom
> and priests to serve our God,
> and they will reign on earth' «
>   (Revelation 5:6 10).

The Bible continues to show us scenes of heaven and scenes in heaven. It says:

THE PRACTICE OF PRAISE

«Then I looked and heard the voice of many angels, numbering thousands upon thousands, and ten thousand times ten thousand. They encircled the throne and the four creatures and the elders. In a loud voice they sang:

'Worthy is the Lamb, who was slain,
to receive power and wealth
and wisdom and strength and honour
and glory and praise!' "
(Revelation 5:11 12).

The Bible continues and says: «Then I heard every creature in heaven and on earth and under the earth and on the sea, and all that is in them, singing:

'To him who sits on the throne and to the Lamb
be praise and honour and glory and power,
for ever and ever!' «
The four living creatures said, 'Amen,' and the elders fell down and worshipped" (Revelation 5:13 14).

The Bible continues to show us scenes in heaven. It says, «After this I looked and there before me was a great multitude that no one could count, from every nation, tribe, people and language, standing before the throne and in front of the Lamb. They were wearing white robes and were holding palm branches in their hands. And they cried out in a loud voice:

'Salvation belongs to our God,
who sits on the throne,
and to the Lamb.'

All the angels were standing round the throne and around
the elders and the four living creatures. They fell down on
their faces before the throne and worshipped God, saying:

'Amen!
Praise and glory
and wisdom and thanks and honour
and power and strength
be to our God for ever and ever.
Amen!' « (Revelation 7:9 12).

We shall look at three more scenes of heaven before we end
this chapter. The Bible says, «The seventh angel sounded his
trumpet, and there were loud voices in heaven, which said:
'The kingdom of the world has become the kingdom of our
Lord and of his Christ; and he will reign for ever!'

And the twenty four elders, who were seated on their thrones
before God, fell on their faces and worshipped God, saying:

'We give thanks to you, Lord God Almighty,
the One who is and who was,
because you have taken your great power
and have begun to reign.
The nations were angry;

and your wrath has come.
The time has come for judging the dead,
and for rewarding your servants the prophets
and your saints and those who reverence your name,
both small and great -
and for destroying those who destroy the earth' «
(Revelation 11:15 18).

The Bible says, «I saw in heaven another great and marvellous sign: seven angels with the last plagues   last, because with them God's wrath is completed. And I saw what looked like a sea of glass mixed with fire and, standing beside the sea, those who had been victorious over the beast and his image and over the number of his name. They held harps given to them by God and sang the song of Moses the servant of God and the song of the Lamb:

'Great and marvellous are your deeds,
Lord God Almighty.
Just and true are your ways,
King of the ages.
Who will not fear you, O Lord,
and bring glory to your name ?
For you alone are holy.
All nations will come
and worship before you,
for your righteous acts have been revealed' «
(Revelation 15:1 4).

One of the last scenes in heaven which has been given to us in the Book is one of praise and thanksgiving. The Bible says: «After this I heard what sounded like the roar of a great multitude in heaven shouting:

> 'Hallelujah!
> Salvation and glory and power belong to our God,
> for true are his judgments.
> He has condemned the great prostitute
> who corrupted the earth by her adulteries.
> He has avenged on her the blood of his servants.'

And again they shouted:

> 'Hallelujah!
> The smoke from her goes up for ever and ever.'

The twenty four elders and the four living creatures fell down and worshipped God, who was seated on the throne. And they cried: 'Amen, Hallelujah!'

Then a voice came from the throne, saying:

> 'Praise our God,
> all you his servants,
> you who fear him,
> both small and great!'

Then I heard what sounded like a great multitude, like

the roar of rushing waters and like loud peals of thunder, shouting:

> 'Hallelujah!
> For our Lord God Almighty reigns.
> Let us rejoice and be glad
> and give him glory!
> For the wedding of the Lamb has come,
> and his bride has made herself ready.
> Fine linen, bright and clean,
> was given to her to wear' «
>
> (Revelation 19:1 8).

Praising and thanking God shall be the pre occupation of the saints in glory. One hymn writer puts it this way:

> Jesus, we come to Thee,
> Oh, take us in!
> Set Thou our spirits free;
> Cleanse us from sin!
> Then, in yon land of light,
> Clothed in our robes of white
> Resting not day nor night,
> Thee we will sing.
> (Sacred Songs and Solos No. 281)

Another hymn writer wrote:

Hark! hark! the song the ransomed sing,
A new made song of praise;
The Lord the Lamb they glorify,
And these the strains they raise:
«Glory to Him who loved us,
And washed us in His blood;
Who cleansed our souls from guilt and sin,
By that pure, living flood!»
(Sacred Songs and Solos No.999).

Yet another hymn writer wrote:

«Who are these, whose songs are sounding,
O'er the golden harps above?»
Hark! they tell of grace abounding,
And Jehovah's sovereign love.
«These are they...who washed their robes...
and made them white...in the blood of the Lamb.»
(Sacred Songs and Solos No.1003).

An unknown hymn writer wrote:

When we've been there ten thousand years,
Bright shining as the sun,
We'll have no less days,
To sing God's praise,
Than when we first began.

Yes, heaven shall be for praising and thanking the Lord, and the best place to start preparing and mastering the occupation of heaven is here on earth, and the best time to major in it is today.

Amen.

THANK YOU FOR READING THIS BOOK

If you have any question and/or need help, do not hesitate to contact us through **ztfbooks@cmfionline.org**. If the book has blessed you, then we would also be grateful if you leave a positive review at your favorite (online) retailer.

ZTF BOOKS, through Christian Publishing House (CPH) offers a wide selection of best selling Christian books (in print-POD, eBook & audiobook formats) on a broad spectrum of topics, including marriage & family, sexuality, practical spiritual warfare, Christian service, Christian leadership, and much more. Visit us at **www.ztfbooks.com** to learn more about our latest releases and special offers. **And thank you for being a ZTF BOOK reader.**

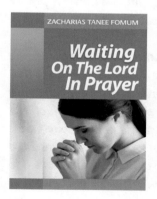

We would like to recommend to you the next book in This Series.

**Waiting
On the Lord
In Prayer**

For many believers, prayer is coming to the Lord and throwing as many requests to Him as possible in the shortest possible time, and then rushing away. The next time, the same process may be repeated with other requests added, while some of the previous ones may be forgotten. This is unfortunate.

God ordained prayer primarily so that His needs be met. In the prayer that the Lord Jesus taught his disciples, the priority of prayer was to be His Name, His Kingdom, and His Will. «Our Father in heaven, hallowed be your name, your kingdom come, your will be done on earth as it is in heaven. Give us today our daily bread. Forgive us our debts, as we also have forgiven our debtors. And lead us not into temptation, but deliver us from the evil one» (Matthew 6:9-13). If the priority in prayer are His name; His kingdom and His will, then it is obvious that for anyone to pray to the satisfaction of God, that one must come before God and wait before God, so that God should give him revelations as to what the needs of His Name, His Kingdom and His Will are. Until these are revealed by God to man, man cannot pray rightly. After they are revealed to man, man can begin to pray what God would have him pray about. This makes waiting on the Lord in prayer a must; for without waiting on the Lord in prayer there is no other way by which these things can be known.

The other issue is that we do not know what our real needs are. We may think that we know what we need, but a closer look will betray our ignorance. Only God knows what our true needs are. Faced with the issues of choosing a wife or a career, we have to face the fact that although we may know what we need now, we do not know what we shall need five, ten, twenty or fifty years from today. God knows what we shall need all the years of our lives. If we wait on Him to reveal to us what we shall always need so that we can ask what will meet our short and long term needs, then we shall be the happier for it. This again makes waiting on the Lord in prayer a must.

The third thing we want to say is that unless people spend time together, they will not know each other much. Those who want to know the Lord must wait on Him in prayer, so that He may reveal Himself ever increasingly to them. The more a person waits on the Lord, the more the Lord will reveal Himself to that one; and the more revelations the person has from the Lord of His character, His will, His plans, His purposes, etc., the more the person will know the Lord. This again makes waiting on the Lord in prayer a must; for without such waiting, the believer will only have a superficial knowledge of Him.

We send this book out with prayer that the many believers who are being awakened to a life of praying, and are actually praying, learn to wait on the Lord in prayer and so pray more correctly. We send this book out with prayer that since it is a matter of Waiting On The Lord In Prayer, the saints should not just wait in prayer, but they should wait on the Lord in prayer. That is, they should wait and wait and keep waiting until the Lord has spoken or answered.

We are well aware of the fact that as in all aspects of spiritual science there is an initiation, a learning and a continuation as progress is made, those who do not yet wait on the Lord in prayer will enrol in the School Of Waiting On The Lord In Prayer, and make progress. We commend you, dear reader, as we commend this book, to the Lord of glory with prayer that He be glad to use this book for your spiritual enrichment.

CONNECT WITH THE AUTHOR

- **Social media:**

  o Facebook: https://facebook.com/cmfionline,
  o Twitter: http://twitter.com/cmfionline,
  o YouTube: https://www.youtube.com/user/CMFIonline/videos,
  o Instagram: https://www.instagram.com/cmfionline

- **Author website:** https://www.ztfministry.org
- **Online Bookshop:** http://www.cph.ztfministry.org
- **FREE online Bible Course:** http://www.bcc.ztfministry.org
- **Internet Radio:** https://rvc.ztfministry.org
- **Podcast:** https://podcast.ztfministry.org

We equally offer on-ground and remote training courses (all year round) from basic to university level at the

  o **University of Prayer and Fasting (WUPF):**
    http://wupd.ztfministry.org, and
  o **School of Knowing and Serving God (SKSG):**
    http://sksg.ztfministry.org

You are highly welcome to enroll at your soonest convenience. Or maybe our FREE online course (http://bcc.ztfministry.org) will be much handy?

VERY IMPORTANT!!!

If you have not yet received Jesus as your Lord and Saviour, I encourage you to receive Him. Here are some steps to help you,

ADMIT that you are a sinner by nature and by practice and that on your own you are without hope. Tell God you have personally sinned against Him in your thoughts, words and deeds. Confess your sins to Him, one after another in a sincere prayer. Do not leave out any sins that you can remember. Truly turn from your sinful ways and abandon them. If you stole, steal no more. If you have been committing adultery or fornication, stop it. God will not forgive you if you have no desire to stop sinning in all areas of your life, but if you are sincere, He will give you the power to stop sinning.

BELIEVE that Jesus Christ, who is God's Son, is the only Way, the only Truth and the only Life. Jesus said, "I am the way, the truth and the life; no one comes to the Father, but by me" (John 14:6). The Bible says, "For there is one God, and there is one mediator between God and men, the man Christ Jesus, who gave himself as a ransom for all" (1 Timothy 2:5-6). "And there is salvation in no one else (apart from Jesus), for there is no other name under heaven given among men by which we must be saved" (Acts 4:12). But to all who received him, who believed in his name, he gave power to become children of God..." (John 1:12). BUT,

CONSIDER the cost of following Him. Jesus said that all who follow Him must deny themselves, and this includes selfish financial, social and other interests. He also wants

His followers to take up their crosses and follow Him. Are you prepared to abandon your own interests daily for those of Christ? Are you prepared to be led in a new direction by Him? Are you prepared to suffer for Him and die for Him if need be? Jesus will have nothing to do with half-hearted people. His demands are total. He will only receive and forgive those who are prepared to follow Him AT ANY COST. Think about it and count the cost. If you are prepared to follow Him, come what may, then there is something to do.

INVITE Jesus to come into your heart and life. He says, "Behold I stand at the door and knock. If anyone hears my voice and opens the door (to his heart and life), I will come in to him and eat with him, and he with me " (Revelation 3:20). Why don't you pray a prayer like the following one or one of your own construction as the Holy Spirit leads?

> *"Lord Jesus, I am a wretched, lost sinner who has sinned in thought, word and deed. Forgive all my sins and cleanse me. Receive me, Saviour and transform me into a child of God. Come into my heart now and give me eternal life right now. I will follow you at all costs, trusting the Holy Spirit to give me all the power I need."*

When you pray this prayer sincerely, Jesus answers at once and justifies you before God and makes you His child.

*Please write to me (**ztfbooks@cmfionline.org**) and I will pray for you and help you as you go on with Jesus Christ.*

ABOUT THE AUTHOR

Zacharias Tanee FOMUM
1945-2009
Founding Leader,
Christian Missionary Fellowship International
www.cmfionline.org (C.M.F.I)

Professor Zacharias Tanee Fomum (http://www.cmfionline.org/index.php/about-us/our-founder) was born in the flesh on 20th June 1945 and became born again on 13th June 1956. On 1st October 1966, He consecrated his life to the Lord Jesus and to His service, and was filled with the Holy Spirit on 24th October 1970. He was taken to be with the Lord on 14th March, 2009.

Pr Fomum was admitted to a first class in the Bachelor of Science degree, graduating as a prize winning student from Fourah Bay College in the University of Sierra Leone in October 1969. At the age of 28, he was awarded a Ph.D. in Organic Chemistry by the University of Makerere, Kampala in Uganda. In October 2005, he was awarded a Doctor of Science (D.Sc) by the University of Durham, Great Britain. This higher doctorate was in recognition of his distinct contributions to scientific knowledge through research. As a Professor of Organic Chemistry in the University of Yaounde 1, Cameroon, Professor Fomum supervised or co-supervised more than 100 Master's Degree and Doctoral Degree theses and co-authored over 160 scientific articles in leading international journals. He considered Jesus Christ the Lord of Science ("For by Him all things were created..." – Colossians 1:16), and scientific research an act of obedience to God's command to "subdue the earth" (Genesis 1:28). He therefore made the Lord Jesus the Director of his research laboratory while he took the place of deputy director, and attributed his outstanding success as a scientist to Jesus' revelational leadership.

In more than 40 years of Christian ministry, Pr Fomum travelled extensively, preaching the Gospel, planting churches and training spiritual leaders. He made more than:

- 700 missionary journeys within Cameroon, which ranged from one day to three weeks in duration.

- 500 missionary journeys to more than 70 different nations in all the six continents. These ranged from two days to six weeks in duration.

By the time of his going to be with the Lord in 2009, he had preached in over 1000 localities in Cameroon, sent over 200 national missionaries into many localities in Cameroon and planted over 1300 churches in the various administrative provinces of Cameroon. At his base in Yaounde, he planted and built a mega-church with his co-workers which grew to a steady membership of about 12,000. Pr Fomum was the founding team-leader of Christian Missionary Fellowship International (CMFI); an evangelism, soul-winning, disciple making, Church-planting and missionary-sending movement with more than 200 international missionaries and thousands of churches in 65 nations spread across Africa, Europe, the Americas, Asia and Oceania. In the course of their ministry, Pr Fomum and his team witnessed more than 10,000 recorded healing miracles performed by God in answer to prayer in the name of Jesus Christ. These miracles include instant healings of headaches, cancers, HIV/AIDS, blindness, deafness, dumbness, paralysis, madness, and new teeth and organs received.

Pr Fomum read the entire Bible more than 60 times, read more than 1350 books on the Christian faith and authored over 150 books to advance the Gospel of Jesus Christ. 5 million copies of these books are in circulation in 12 languages as well as 16 million gospel tracts in 17 languages. Pr Fomum was a man who sought God. He spent between 15 minutes and six hours daily alone with God in what he called Daily Dynamic Encounters with God (DDEWG). During these DDEWG he read God's Word, meditated on it, listened to God's voice, heard God speak to him, recorded what God was saying to him and prayed it through. He thus had over 18,000 DDEWG. He also had over 60 periods of withdrawing to seek God alone for periods that ranged from 3 to 21 days (which he termed Retreats for Spiritual Progress). The time he spent seeking God slowly transformed him into a man who hungered, thirsted and panted after God. His unceasing heart cry was: "Oh, that I would have more of God!"

Pr Fomum was a man of prayer and a leading teacher on prayer in many churches and conferences around the world. He considered prayer to be the most important work that can be done for God and for man. He was a man of faith who believed that God answers prayer. He kept a record of his prayer requests and had over 50, 000 recorded answers to prayer in his prayer books. He carried out over 100 Prayer

Walks of between five and forty-seven kilometres in towns and cities around the world. He and his team carried out over 57 Prayer Crusades (periods of forty days and nights during which at least eight hours are invested into prayer each day). They also carried out over 80 Prayer Sieges (times of near non-stop praying that ranges from 24 hours to 120 hours). He authored the Prayer Power Series, a 13-volume set of books on various aspects of prayer; Supplication, Fasting, Intercession and Spiritual Warfare. He started prayer chains, prayer rooms, prayer houses, national and continental prayer movements in Cameroon and other nations. He worked with leaders of local churches in India to disciple and train more than 2 million believers.

Pr Fomum also considered fasting as one of the weapons of Christian Spiritual Warfare. He carried out over 250 fasts ranging from three days to forty days, drinking only water or water supplemented with soluble vitamins. Called by the Lord to a distinct ministry of intercession, he pioneered fasting and prayer movements and led in battles against principalities and powers obstructing the progress of the Gospel and God's global purposes. He was enabled to carry out 3 supra – long fasts of between 52 and 70 days in his final years.

Pr Fomum chose a lifestyle of simplicity and "self- imposed poverty" in order to invest more funds into the critical work of evangelism, soulwinning, church-planting and the building up of believers. Knowing the importance of money and its role in the battle to reach those without Christ with the glorious Gospel, he and his wife grew to investing 92.5% of their earned income from all sources (salaries, allowances, royalties and cash gifts) into the Gospel. They invested with the hope that, as they grew in the knowledge and the love of the Lord, and the perishing souls of people, they would one day invest 99% of their income into the Gospel.

He was married to Prisca Zei Fomum and they had seven children who are all involved in the work of the Gospel, some serving as missionaries. Prisca is a national and international minister, specializing in the winning and discipling of children to Jesus Christ. She also communicates and imparts the vision of ministry to children with a view to raising and building up ministers to them.

The Professor owed all that he was and all that God had done through him, to the unmerited favour and blessing of God and to his worldwide army of friends and co-workers. He considered himself nothing without them and the blessing of God; and would have amounted to nothing but for them.

All praise and glory to Jesus Christ!

OTHER BOOKS
FROM THE AUTHOR

THE CHRISTIAN
WAY SERIES

1. The Way Of Life
2. The Way Of Obedience
3. The Way Of Discipleship
4. The Way Of Sanctification
5. The Way Of Christian Character
6. The Way Of Spiritual Power
7. The Way Of Christian Service
8. The Way Of Spiritual Warfare
9. The Way Of Suffering For Christ
10. The Way Of Victorious Praying
11. The Way Of Overcomers
12. The Way Of Spiritual Encouragement
13. The Way Of Loving The Lord

THE PRAYER
POWER SERIES

1. The Way Of Victorious Praying
2. The Ministry Of Fasting
3. The Art Of Intercession
4. The Practice Of Intercession
5. Praying With Power
6. Practical Spiritual Warfare Through Prayer
7. Moving God Through Prayer
8. The Ministry Of Praise And Thanksgiving
9. Waiting On The Lord In Prayer
10. The Ministry Of Supplication
11. Life-Changing Thoughts On Prayer, Volume 1
12. The Centrality Of Prayer
13. Spiritual Aggressiveness
14. Life-Changing Thoughts On Prayer, Volume 2
15. Prayer and Spiritual Intimacy
16. Life-Changing Thoughts on Prayer Volume 3
17. The Art of Worship

THE PRACTICAL HELPS FOR
OVERCOMERS SERIES

1. Discipleship at any cost
2. The Use Of Time
3. Retreats For Spiritual Progress
4. Personal Spiritual Revival
5. Daily Dynamic Encounters With God
6. The School Of Truth
7. How To Succeed In The Christian Life
8. The Christian And Money
9. Deliverance From The Sin Of Laziness
10. The Art Of Working Hard
11. Knowing God - The Greatest Need Of The Hour
12. Revelation: A Must
13. True Repentance
14. Restitution - An Important Message For The Overcomers
15. You Can Receive A Pure Heart Today
16. You Can Lead Someone To The Lord Jesus Today
17. You Can Receive The Baptism Into The Holy Spirit Now
18. The Dignity Of Manual Labour
19. You Have A Talent!
20. The Making Of Disciples
21. The Secret Of Spiritual Fruitfulness
22. Are You Still A Disciple Of The Lord Jesus?
23. The Overcomer As A Servant Of Man

THE GOD, SEX AND YOU
SERIES

1. Enjoying The Premarital Life
2. Enjoying The Choice Of Your Marriage Partner

3. Enjoying The Married Life
4. Divorce And Remarriage
5. A Successful Marriage; The Husband's Making
6. A Successful Marriage; The Wife's Making

THE ZTF NEW BOOKS SERIES

1. Power For Service
2. The Art Of Worship
3. Issues Of The Heart
4. In The Crucible For Service
5. Spiritual Nobility
6. Roots And Destinies
7. Revolutionary Thoughts On Spiritual Leadership
8. The Leader And His God
9. The Overthrow Of Principalities And Powers
10. Walking With God
11. God Centeredness
12. Victorious Dispositions
13. The Believer's Conscience
14. The Processes Of Faith
15. Spiritual Gifts
16. The Missionary As A Son
17. You, Your Team And Your Ministry
18. Prayer And A Walk With God
19. Leading A Local Church
20. Church Planting Strategies
21. The Character And The Personality of The Leader
22. Deliverance From The Sin of Gluttony
23. The Spirit Filled Life
24. The Church: Rights And Responsibilities Of The Believer
25. Thoughts On Marriage
26. Learning To Importune In Prayer
27. Jesus Saves And Heals Today
28. God, Money And You
29. Meet The Liberator
30. Salvation And Soul Winning
31. The Salvation Of The Lord Jesus: Soul Winning (Vol. 3)
32. Soul Winning And The Making Of Disciples
33. Victorious Soul Winning
34. Making Spiritual Progress (Vol. 4)
35. Life Changing Thought On Prayer (Vol. 3)
36. Knowing God And Walking With Him
37. What Our Ministry Is
38. Practical Dying To Self And The Spirit-filled Life
39. Leading God's People
40. Laws Of Spiritual Leadership
41. From His Lips: Compilation of Autobiographical Notes on Professor Zacharias Tanee Fomum
42. The School of Soul Winners and Soul Winning
43. The Complete Work of Zacharias Tanee Fomum on Prayer (Volume 1)
44. Knowing and Serving God (Volume 2)
45. Walking With God (Volume 1)

THE PRACTICAL HELPS IN SANCTIFICATION SERIES

1. Deliverance From Sin
2. The Way Of Sanctification
3. Sanctified And Consecrated For Spiritual Ministry
4. The Sower, The Seed And The Hearts Of Men
5. Freedom From The Sin Of Adultery And Fornication
6. The Sin Before You May Lead To Immediate Death: Do Not Commit It!
7. Be Filled With The Holy Spirit
8. The Power Of The Holy Spirit In The Winning Of The Lost

THE MAKING SPIRITUAL PROGRESS SERIES

1. Vision, Burden, Action
2. The Ministers And The Ministry of The New Covenant
3. The Cross In The Life And Ministry Of The Believer
4. Knowing The God Of Unparalleled Goodness
5. Brokenness: The Secret Of Spiritual

Overflow
6. The Secret Of Spiritual Rest
7. Making Spiritual Progress, Volume 1
8. Making Spiritual Progress, Volume 2
9. Making Spiritual Progress, Volume 3
10. Making Spiritual Progress, Volume 4

THE EVANGELISM SERIES

1. God's Love And Forgiveness
2. The Way Of Life
3. Come Back Home My Son; I Still Love You
4. Jesus Loves You And Wants To Heal You
5. Come And See; Jesus Has Not Changed!
6. 36 Reasons For Winning The Lost To Christ
7. Soul Winning, Volume 1
8. Soul Winning, Volume 2
9. Celebrity A Mask

THE OTHER BOOKS SERIES

1. Laws Of Spiritual Success, Volume 1
2. The Shepherd And The Flock
3. Deliverance From Demons
4. Inner Healing
5. No Failure Needs To Be Final
6. Facing Life's Problems Victoriously
7. A Word To The Students
8. The Prophecy Of The Overthrow Of The Satanic Prince Of Cameroon
9. Basic Christian Leadership
10. A Missionary life and a missionary heart
11. Power to perform miracles

THE WOMEN OF THE GLORY SERIES

1. The Secluded Worshipper: The Life, Ministry, And Glorification Of The Prophetess Anna
2. Unending Intimacy: The Transformation, Choices And Overflow of Mary of Bethany

3. Winning Love: The rescue, development and fulfilment of Mary Magdalene
4. Not Meant for Defeat: The Rise, Battles, and Triumph of Queen Esther

THE ANTHOLOGY SERIES

1. The School of Soul Winners and Soul Winning
2. The Complete Works of Zacharias Tanee Fomum on Prayer (Volume 1)
3. The Complete Works of Zacharias Tanee Fomum on Leadership (Volume 1)
4. The Complete Works of Z.T Fomum on Marriage
5. Making Spiritual Progress (The Complete Box Set of Four Volumes)

THE OTHER BOOKS SERIES

1. A Broken Vessel
2. The Joy of Begging to Belong to the Lord Jesus Christ: A Testimony

THE BIOGRAPHICAL SERIES

1. From His Lips: ZT Fomum - About himself
2. From His Lips: ZT Fomum - About His Co-Workers
3. From His Lips: ZT Fomum - About His Missions
4. From His Lips: ZT Fomum - About His Work
5. From His Lips: Z.T. Fomum - School of Knowing & Serving God